The History And Antiquities Of The See And Cathedral Church Of Winchester ...: Including Biographical Anecdotes Of The Bishops, And Of Other Eminent Persons Connected With The Church

John Britton

Engraved by H. Le Keux, from a Drawing by John Blore, for Britton's History &c of Winchester Cathedral.

WINCHESTER CATHEDRAL CHURCH.
Part of the Stalls of the Choir.
London, Published Dec.r 2 1816. by Longman & C.o Paternoster Row.
Printed by Mc.Queen.

The History and Antiquities of the Cathedral Church of WINCHESTER Illustrated with Views Plans Sections Details &c.

Engraved by R. L. Hind, from a Drawing by Edw. Blore, for Britton's History &c. of Winchester Cathedral.

WINCHESTER CATHEDRAL CHURCH.
Part of the Stalls of the Choir
London. Published Dec.r 1, 1816, by Longman &c.a Paternoster Row.

Printed by Hayward

THE

HISTORY AND ANTIQUITIES

OF THE

SEE AND CATHEDRAL CHURCH

OF

𝔚𝔦𝔫𝔠𝔥𝔢𝔰𝔱𝔢𝔯;

ILLUSTRATED WITH

A SERIES OF ENGRAVINGS,

OF

𝔙𝔦𝔢𝔴𝔰, 𝔈𝔩𝔢𝔟𝔞𝔱𝔦𝔬𝔫𝔰, 𝔓𝔩𝔞𝔫𝔰, 𝔞𝔫𝔡 𝔇𝔢𝔱𝔞𝔦𝔩𝔰 𝔬𝔣 𝔱𝔥𝔢 𝔄𝔯𝔠𝔥𝔦𝔱𝔢𝔠𝔱𝔲𝔯𝔢 𝔬𝔣 𝔱𝔥𝔞𝔱 𝔈𝔡𝔦𝔣𝔦𝔠𝔢:

INCLUDING

BIOGRAPHICAL ANECDOTES OF THE BISHOPS,

AND OF

OTHER EMINENT PERSONS CONNECTED WITH THE CHURCH.

BY

JOHN BRITTON, F.S.A.

𝔏𝔬𝔫𝔡𝔬𝔫:

PRINTED FOR, AND PUBLISHED BY, LONGMAN, HURST, REES, ORME, AND BROWN,
PATERNOSTER ROW;
THE AUTHOR, 10, TAVISTOCK PLACE; AND J. TAYLOR, 59, HIGH HOLBORN.

1817.

C. Whittingham, Printer, Chiswick.

PREFACE.

SINCE the preceding dedication was published, the whole English nation has had to deplore and lament the sudden and melancholy death of the amiable Princess to whom it was addressed. Never, perhaps, was there a more general and unanimous sympathy excited : never were all parties and all classes of people more agreed as to the eligibility of a future sovereign,—as to the domestic virtues of the wife, and as to the incalculable influence of such qualities on the fashion and manners of a country. Let us cherish, however, an ardent hope, that the esteem she excited will act as a stimulus to other heirs to the crown ;—for the greatest treasure a monarch can obtain is a nation's love. Splendid and costly monuments may be raised—churches may be founded—and poets may eulogise the wealthy and the great—but neither of those will secure the impartial approbation of the honest historian, if not accompanied by real worth, or talents. In examining the monuments of our Cathedrals, we are often disgusted with the fulsome flattery and falsehood of many inscriptions ;—we often see the short-sighted policy of those who seek to obtain posthumous fame by testamentary legacies and foundations : and have frequent occasion to deplore that the names, characters, and worldly situations of real benefactors to mankind, are often unnoticed by marble tablets and sepulchral eulogia. In the present age, however, real merit is very generally understood and appreciated; and great talents, if united with integrity, will certainly be honoured and perpetuated. It is a noble and proud characteristic of the English, to cherish and respect connubial happiness; to admire domestic virtues; and wherever these are rendered apparent, they immediately secure the sincerest and warmest sympathy. A people so constituted must be dignified in the scale of nations; and Englishmen, whilst they are proud of their country, should exert their talents to exalt it, and guard its honour with the most watchful jealousy.

Intimately connected as the diocess of Winchester has been with the history and progress of Christianity in England;—with the contentions between the episcopal and monarchial supremacy, I have been seduced into a more extended review of those subjects than will, perhaps, be agreeable to the general reader : but I could not with propriety neglect to notice them, nor yet contract my comments within a smaller compass. On these points I have most scrupulously endeavoured to be candid and strictly impartial ; detailing the opinions of those writers who appear to be most deserving of credit, and occasionally, but rarely, submitting my own. Aware that the civil and ecclesiastical history of Winchester has been amply and learnedly developed by its local historian, and that, from the religious opinions entertained by the writer, much warm, and rather acrimonious, controversy has been produced; my endeavour has been to avoid the intemperate zeal of both parties *. History, antiquity, art, and matter

* See Preface to " *The History, &c. of Norwich Cathedral*," for my opinions on this point.

of fact, are the objects of the present work; not theory, opinion, or romance:—these are fleeting and transitory; may be esteemed to-day, but despised to-morrow: whilst those are lasting: at once affording a gratifying reward to investigation, and permanent satisfaction to the mind.

With the same feelings and principles I have eagerly endeavoured to elucidate the styles and dates of the different parts of Winchester Cathedral. If I have erred in opinion, in statement, or inference, I shall feel thankful for better information, or for friendly correction. Many points, I am willing to admit, are unsettled, and therefore liable to varied interpretations: but I suspect that many persons, with the best intentions, and with well informed minds, are too prone to yield to the seductions of theory and prepossession. Though much has been written and published on this subject, I am persuaded that much more remains to be done; and that we shall never elicit the whole truth, nor come to the arcana of antiquarian science, but by diligent and fastiduous investigation. To elucidate all the nice varieties and gradations of architecture, we must be furnished with the most accurate elevations, sections, and details of ancient buildings; and at length we have a few artists capable of rendering us this invaluable service.

It is the duty of a writer not only to avail himself of all the labours of his predecessors, but to correct their errors and supply their deficiencies. In doing this, however, he should be governed by rigid impartiality, and a manly courage to point out, without exulting at their defects. Knowing the difficulty of attaining truth, he should be lenient and liberal, and his grand rule of action is to be just to himself and to his reader. With these sentiments impressed on the heart, I have penned the following pages; and though they may not comprise all the information that may be required by the critical reader; and though not so full of comments on the errors and mis-statements of preceding writers as some may wish, yet I hope the impartial antiquary will forgive me for the latter omission, and excuse me for the former.

It is now my pleasing task to thank the following correspondents for much useful communication and kindnesses—the DEAN of WINCHESTER; the Rev. E. POULTER; the Rev. H. LEE; the Rev. F. IREMONGER; B. WINTER, Esq.; the Rev. R. YATES; WM. GARBETT, Esq.; and WM. HAMPER, Esq.

Having completed the history and illustration of Winchester Cathedral, being the third of this series, I shall next proceed to illustrate and elucidate that of YORK, for which nearly the whole of the drawings are completed by Messrs. Blore and Mackenzie. From the progress made, I have reason to believe that the whole work will be completed in the course of twelve months; and I cannot doubt but that the historical and architectural materials, relating to this metropolitical church, will abound with curious and interesting facts. The architecture is replete with beautiful forms and features, and the whole will be amply and accurately displayed by the faithful pencils of the artists above-named.

History and Antiquities

OF

WINCHESTER CATHEDRAL CHURCH.

Chap. I.

FIRST ESTABLISHMENT OF CHRISTIANITY IN BRITAIN:—INQUIRY INTO THE REALITY AND SOVEREIGNTY OF LUCIUS:—ESTABLISHMENT OF A SEE AT WINCHESTER:—THE EXTENT AND INFLUENCE OF ITS DOMINION:— HISTORY OF THE FOUNDATION AND SUCCESSIVE ALTERATIONS OF THE CATHEDRAL, THROUGH THE DYNASTY OF THE KINGS OF THE WEST SAXONS TO THE PERIOD OF THE NORMAN CONQUEST.

It is not easy, nor would it be desirable, to examine the Cathedral of Winchester without connecting it with eminent men and memorable events of former ages. Its history, indeed, is intimately blended with that of the nation; and its annals embrace many facts and relations which cannot fail to interest the feelings of the philosopher, the Christian, the historian, and the antiquary. As connected with the disputable and uncertain primary establishment of Christianity in Britain—as the temple wherein its benign doctrines were promulgated to Britons and Romans— and as the place of coronation and sepulture of Anglo-Saxon and Anglo-Norman monarchs, the Cathedral of Winchester is eminently important. In reviewing its early history we are, however, constantly perplexed in the mazes of fable, tradition, and probable narrative; and feel extreme difficulty in discriminating the one from the other, and rendering our account rational, satisfactory, and authentic. From the earliest period to the dissolution of the monastic institutions in Great Britain, Winchester appears to have been a place of local and national consequence. Under the Celtic or Belgic Britons, here was certainly a town called *Caer-Gwent,* or the White City: this was subsequently occupied, fortified, and rendered a permanent station by the Romans, and denominated by them *Venta-Belgarum.* By the West Saxons it was made their chief seat, and it afterwards became the metropolis of all England. The Norman monarchs and some subsequent kings either resided at, or conferred certain marks of distinction on the city. Hence we shall find that, in its political and ecclesiastical history, there are abundant subjects for interesting inquiry and for extended disquisition. On the present occasion, however, it will be necessary to confine our attention to the latter subject.

The early history of WINCHESTER CATHEDRAL has been connected, by the almost general assent of topographical writers, with the very introduction of Christianity itself into this island; yet so few and meagre are the notices which the records of antiquity furnish on the subject, and so much are they intermingled with fiction and improbabilities, that the impartial inquirer must still remain in a state of dubiety as to the real facts. The most effective research cannot now supply enough evidence to determine the true origin of this Church; and however gratifying to curiosity it would be to discover the dates of its foundation and successive enlargements, it has become impossible to do so from the want of authentic documents. The traditionary legends of monkish writers are utterly insufficient to satisfy the judgment of any historian, in whose breast the love of truth is more powerful than a slavish attachment to hypothesis; yet we have scarcely any other data on which to ground the annals of the first ages of this See and Cathedral.

The first conversion of the Britons to Christianity, though in its consequences of such vast and incalculable importance, is involved in the greatest obscurity; as well in regard to the exact time at which it took place, as to the real persons by whom, or under whose auspices, that conversion was effected. Ireneus[1], Eusebius[2], and Theodoret[3], have been considered as furnishing competent testimony, " that some of the Apostles visited the British Isles, and that the Britons were among the nations which were converted by the Apostles." The particular persons to whom this honour is generally given, are St. Peter and St. Paul; but, without entering into the questionable testimony by which this opinion has been supported, it will be sufficient in this place to remark, generally, that Cardinal Baronius and other Roman Catholic writers ascribe the promulgation of Christianity in this island to St. Peter; whilst, on the contrary, many Protestant writers maintain that the Gospel was first preached here by St. Paul: of this latter opinion is the learned Dr. Burgess, Bishop of St. David's, who, in a Sermon, intituled " The first Seven Epochs of the ancient British Church[4]," asserts the probability of St. Paul having accompanied the family of Caractacus from Rome, about the year 58; and this conjecture (founded on different passages in the ancient historians and fathers of the Church), the worthy prelate considers to be substantiated by a record in the British Triads[5], where it is said " that the father of Caractacus went to Rome as an hostage for his son, and others of his family; that he staid there seven years; and that on his return he brought the knowledge of Christianity to his countrymen from Rome."—" It is a remarkable and very interesting fact," continues the bishop, " that the detention of the British hostages should have been coincident with St. Paul's residence there as a prisoner; and it was a not less favourable coincidence, that they should be released from confinement in the same year in which St. Paul was set at liberty. Nothing could be more convenient for St. Paul's mission to the Gentiles, than the opportunity which their return must have afforded him of introducing the gospel into

---

[1] Iren. *lib.* i. *cap.* 2, 3.　　　　　　[2] Euseb. *lib.* iii. *cap.* 7. *p.* 113.

[3] Theod. *tom.* iv. *serm.* 9, *p.* 611.　　[4] Printed in 1813, 8vo.

[5] Some of these ancient documents are published in the *Myvyrian Archæology*, and are partly translated in Williams's Dissertation on the *Pelagian Heresy*, p. 14; and by Mr. Roberts, in the Appendix to his *Collectanea Cambrica*, p. 203.

Britain; and nothing more probable than that he should readily embrace such an opportunity."

Notwithstanding the plausibility of this argument, it seems evident that, had St. Paul really visited Britain, a more direct testimony of the fact would have been found than a few obscure passages in the ancient fathers; and though in his Epistle to the Romans, (chap. 15.) St. Paul twice mentions his intention of going into Spain, yet it is very problematical whether that purpose was ever carried into effect. The total silence also of the Roman historians, as to any Christian hierarchy being established in this island, during the three first centuries of the Roman dominion here (since it appears from Ignatius that there could have been no church without a succession of bishops[6]), affords a strong presumption that, during the above period, the diffusion of Christianity in Britain was extremely limited; and that it arose more from accidental circumstances than from a settled plan of conversion.

The gradual spread of the gospel in Italy and Gaul, and the intercourse maintained between the imperial seat of Rome and its dependencies, were unquestionably the leading causes of the introduction of Christianity into Britain; yet the attributing of that event, personally, either to St. Paul or to Lucius, a British king, who is said to have been seated at Venta, or Winchester, and to have reigned between the years 164 and 190, appears neither to be warranted by historical records nor probability.

That there were certain individuals among the Britons who, in the first century after Christ, embraced the pure doctrines which he taught is evident, both from Tacitus and Martial. The former states, in his Annals[7], that a distinguished British lady, named Pomponia Græcina, a Christian, and the wife of Aulus Plautius (who had been pro-prætor of the Roman province in this island), was prosecuted (A. D. 57), and in danger of losing her life for her religion; and the latter, in two Epigrams[8], brings us acquainted with the virtues and beauty of Claudia Rufina, another Christian female of noble birth, who was also a native

---

[6] Igna. Epist. ad Trall. § 3.   [7] *Lib.* xiii. *cap.* 32.

[8] *Lib.* iv. *Ep.* 13; and *lib.* xi. *Ep.* 54.

of this island, and who was married to a senator of Rome, named Rufus Pudens. This lady and her husband are generally admitted to have been the persons of whom St. Paul speaks as Christians, and whose greetings he sends to Timothy, in that epistle[9] which he wrote when going to appear a second time before Nero, previously to his martyrdom in June, A.D. 66. The influence of these ladies would most probably be exerted to extend the knowledge of the Christian dispensation in their own country; yet we have the positive evidence of Pliny, as to the fact of the Druidical superstitions of Britain being extremely prevalent, even so late as fifty years after the death of Claudius, and although several edicts had been issued against Druidism by the Roman emperors: his words are " Britannia hodieque eam attonite celebrat, tantis ceremoniis, ut dedisse Persis videri possit;" that is, ' the Britons of this day are accustomed to use and follow it, with such admiration and as many ceremonies, as though they had first taught it unto the Persians'[10].

The most respectable of our ancient writers who mentions the conversion of Lucius and the Britons under his dominion, is Venerable Bede, whom Godwin presumes to have " obtained his information out of the old Martyrologies"[11]. He says, that " In the year of Christ's Incarnation, 156, Marcus Antoninus Verus, the fourteenth emperor from Augustus, began his government with Aurelius Commodus, his brother; in whose time Eleutherius, a holy man, sitting bishop of the Roman Church, Lucius, a king of the Britons, writ unto him his letters, praying that by his appointment and direction he might be made a Christian; and presently he obtained the effect of his godly desire: from which period until the reign of Dioclesian, the Britons inviolably held the true faith, uncorrupted, in peace and quietness[12]."

Such is the simple ground-work of the story of Lucius; but the legends of the monkish annalists of later days have rendered the whole incredible,

[9] 2 Tim. *chap.* iv. v. 21.

[10] In Vita Claud. *cap.* xxv.—Vide Godwin de Præsul. *cap.* iii.   [11] Godwin, ib.

[12] Bede's " Hist. Eccles. Gent. Ang. Lib. Quin. Edit." by Smith. p. 44.

by the absurd and even impossible circumstances which they have thought proper to attach to it. The "*true* Roman Martyrology," as Baronius calls it (although a prior Martyrology, written by Usuardus, at the command of *Carolus Magnus*, about the year 800, mentions nothing concerning Lucius), states that Eleutherius sent the two prelates, Fugatius, and Damianus or Duvianus, into Britain, and that they baptized Lucius and his queen, "and, in a manner, all the people of the land[13]." But the extensive nature of this conversion (as told us by the monks), will be better understood from the following succinct statement, which Bishop Godwin has inserted in the ' Discourse,' prefixed to his ' Catalogue of the Bishops of England'[14].

" Whensoever it was that this good Prince received the faith of Christ: so it fell out (our historians say), that not only his wife and family accompanied him in that happy course, but nobles also and commons, priests and people, high and low, even all the people of this land which we now call England: and that generally all their idols were then defaced, the temples of them being converted into churches for the service of God ; the livings of the idolatrous priests appointed for the maintenance of the priests of the gospel, and that, instead of the twenty-five flamines or high-priests of their idols, there were ordained twenty-five bishops; as also for three arch-flamines, three archbishops ; whereof one was seated at London, another at Yorke, and a third at Carlion in Monmouthshire."— In a subsequent page the bishop says, " It is recorded by most of our writers (in a manner all), that King Lucius, having founded many churches, and afforded unto them many possessions with great privileges, he at last departed this life in peace, and was buried at Gloucester, the fourteenth yeare after his baptism, as some say ; the tenth, as other; and againe (as some other will have it), the fourth."

Such is the substance of the traditions which an inquirer into the

---

[13] "—— ac totum fere populum." In 7 Kal. Jun. The old History of Llandaff, commonly called the Book of St. Teilo, says, that then ames of the messengers sent by Lucius to Eleutherius, were Elvanus and Meduinus, and that the former was constituted a bishop by Eleutherius, and the latter a doctor or teacher, in respect of their eloquence and knowledge in the Scriptures.

[14] *Chap.* iii. *p.* 22. and *p.* 35. Edit. 1615.

church antiquities of Winchester has to examine, before he can obtain any foundation for the erection of genuine history. As the stream of time has rolled on, it is curious to observe how greatly the minute rill of information, given us by Bede, has been amplified in succeeding ages; not, however, from springs " pure and undefiled," but from sources which obscure and blacken the original current.   Rudborne, a monk of Winchester, who lived about the middle of the fifteenth century, and whose history, or annals, of this cathedral has been published by Wharton, in his " Anglia Sacra," affords a very curious illustration of the above remark ; for he has not only strung together the various legendary accounts of former writers, but has added particulars that are not to be found in any preceding historian.   The very singular phraseology in which he has enveloped his narrative, may be judged of from the following translation of the first chapter of his History, as published by Wharton.

" Lucius, the glorious Prince of Britain, being invested with power and the regal diadem, hearing the report of Christianity, far transcending every mode of human estimation, with much charitable zeal, desired that himself and his kingdom, and every people subjected to him, should be instructed in that soul-saving doctrine.   In the first year of his reign he sent certain legates and learned nuncios to the Pope, seeking peace and perpetual health, and also that he would shed a beam of the freely-granted river from the celestial fountain of Christ, the Eternal Sun, to their Prince, sighing for eternal life.   At that time the blessed Father Eleutherius was presiding in all the world, who, from the blessed St. Peter, the prince of the Apostles, was the twelfth in succession to the Apostolical chair.   The most serene Prince Lucius followed up the effect of his most desired proposition.   Now the above mentioned was Eleutherius, the Holy,

> " Who held the Key of Heaven from pole to pole,
> Who, by God's permission, loosened the fetters of the world,
> And unlocked the celestial regions to the pious.

"About the year of the Dominical Incarnation 164, as writeth the Venerable Bede in his ' *De Gestis Anglorum*,' *lib.* i. *cap.* 4. and Martin in his Chronicles, and Gildas the Historian (the Ancient British writer), *lib.* i. *cap.* 7. two learned priests, religious men and monks, named Faganus and Duvianus, with many of their associate monks, were presented to the king; and this prince and all his people were baptized"[15].—

Although Rudborne has cited Gildas as one of his authorities for referring the conversion of Lucius to the year 164, yet the short work, "*De Excidio Britanniæ*," which we have in print of that writer, makes not the least mention of that prince; nor is there any writing of his, now known to be extant, which refers to him. The date too, as given by Rudborne, is manifestly wrong, since Eleutherius did not succeed to the pontificate till after the death of Soter, in 177; but in this the Winchester historian does not stand single; for the learned Usher, as stated by Carte, has collected upwards of twenty different opinions[16], as to the time when Lucius was converted, and held his alleged correspondence with Eleutherius.

Among the arguments employed by Carte, in his extended examination of this question[17], to show that the events, attributed to Lucius, cannot be true, are instanced the very slow progress made by Christianity on this side the Alps, and the non-existence of every kind of credible record relating to a succession of bishops in this island, at any time before the middle of the third century. "No man of learning," says this historian, "however versed in the study of antiquity, or how indefatigable soever in his searches upon this subject, hath ever yet been able to find out so much as the name of any one bishop in Britain, except what are founded upon the legend of Lucius, till after the year 250; the highest point of time to which their succession of bishops ascends in all the sees of Gaul, except Lyons and Vienne;—and the true reason why there was no persecution in this island (as there was in other parts of the Roman empire), till the time of Dioclesian, appears plainly to have been, because till then there were no Christians here considerable enough to be remarked."

Nennius, speaking of Lucius, informs us that after his conversion he

---

[15] Rudborne Hist. Mag. *lib.* i. *cap.* 1.   [16] Antiq. Brit. *cap.* iii. *p.* 20.

[17] Hist. of Eng. *vol.* i. *p.* 132—140.

was called, in allusion to his name, *Lever Maur*, or the *Great Light*, or *Splendour*[18]; and the British Triads[19] are supposed to record the same person by the appellative Lleirwg, or Lles (whence the Latin name, Lucius) who is stated in those documents to have established the first church in Britain, although just before that event is attributed to Bran.

After his conversion, Lucius is said to have made request to Eleutherius for some particulars of the Roman laws, that he might make them a foundation for a settled order of government throughout his own dominions. The answer returned by Eleutherius is supposed, by Bishop Godwin, to have been first recorded " in an old chronicle, entituled *Brutus*, amongst certaine lawes or statutes of the Saxons." There is however much diversity in the copies of this epistle, and some of them have additional sentences. In that published by Usher[20], the date is 169; and the following are the most particular passages, as translated from the Latin, by Godwin :—" Ye require of us the Roman laws and the Emperors to be sent over to you, which you would practice and put in use within your realm. The Roman laws and the Emperors we may ever reprove; but the law of God we may not. Ye have received of late, through God's mercy, in the kingdom of Britain, the law and faith of Christ; ye have with you within the realm both parts of the Scriptures. Out of them, by God's grace, with the council of your realm take ye a law; and by that law, through God's sufferance, rule your kingdom of Britain : for you be God's vicar in your kingdom.—The people and folk of the realm of Britain be yours; whom, if they be divided, ye ought to gather in concord and peace, to call them to the faith and law of Christ, to cherish and to maintain them, to rule and govern them, so as you may keep everlastingly with him whose vicar ye are."

Whatever might be the extent of credulity in prejudiced minds, it is clear to the impartial historian, that the above epistle could never be a genuine one; for the dominion of the Romans had been so extensively spread over this country long prior to the time at which Lucius is said to have swayed the sceptre, that by no possible means could he have been in possession of the enlarged

---

[18] Hist. Brit. c. xviii.　　　[19] See Myvyrian Archaiology.　　　[20] Antiq. Brit.

sovereignty that is thus attributed to him. It is admitted that the Romans grounding their policy on the acknowledged prejudices of human nature, frequently governed their newly-conquered countries by the agency of native kings and princes, and willingly bestowed some portion of regal authority on those who were disposed to sacrifice their independence to ambition. The dominion, however, that was thus delegated by the Romans was always resumed as their conquests became consolidated, and their empire secured. In regard to Britain, wholly subjugated as it was long before the days of Lucius, it would have been utterly inconsistent with every principle of Roman domination to have permitted a native prince to have borne such an extended sway over a country which they had divided into provinces, and placed under the rule of their own præfects. The " *realm of Britain*," could never have been subjected to Lucius; nor does it appear from any Roman author that ever a prince so named was at any time in alliance with them, or was suffered to govern a subordinate kingdom, though even of inferior extent. Still less can we give credence to the legends which attribute the creation of so many archiepiscopal and other Sees to a British king; so long after his country had been subjugated by a foreign power, and upwards of a century before Christianity was protected by the Roman emperors.

From the preceding brief review of the evidence which has been adduced on this controverted subject, it must be clear to the impartial reader, that the story of Lucius is either altogether fabulous, or that Lucius himself was a person whose situation and circumstances in life have been greatly misrepresented. The two coins, mentioned by Archbishop Usher[21], (the one silver, and the other gold, having the figure of a king on them with a cross, and the letters L. V. C.) which have been so frequently referred to in proof that Lucius was both a *King* and a *Christian*, are not so explicitly described as to warrant a belief of the affirmative. The very words, indeed, which the archbishop has employed, says Whitaker, " renders the fact infinitely precarious[22]." He had seen, he affirms, two coins, which

[21] Vide Usher De Prim. *p.* 30, 40.   [22] Hist. of Manchester, *vol.* i. *p.* 405.

were marked with the sign of the cross, " *et Literis obscuriaribusquæ LVC. denotare videbentur;*" a sentence which throws a strong doubt on the presumption of their having been minted by Lucius. It appears from Gildas, also, as quoted by the same historian, that no British king was allowed to coin money after the Roman conquest[23].

The account given by Rudborne, from Moracius, respecting the dimensions of the Cathedral which Lucius is stated to have erected at Winchester, has an equally suspicious air with many of the other circumstances attributed to that personage. It informs us, that " Lucius built a Christian church from the ground," upon a scale of grandeur and magnificence which has never since been equalled;—" its length being 209 paces [about 600 feet], its breadth 80 paces, its height 92 paces, and its width, from one horn [*corner*] across the church to the other, 180 paces;" and that this edifice, when finished, was dedicated in honour of the *Holy Saviour* by Fugatius and Duvianus, who had been sent to Britain from Rome by Pope Eleutherius; and who, likewise, constituted abbot of this place, a monk formerly called *Devotus*[24].

According to the same authority, Lucius bestowed on his new church the privileges of sanctuary, (agreeably to the laws of Dunwallo Malmutius, a reputed British king, said to have lived 500 years before Christ); and also

---

[23] Hist. of Manchester, *vol.* i. *p.* 405.

[24] Rudb. *lib.* i. Rudborne's words are these:—" *Abbatemque loci constituerunt Monachum quendam vocabulo Devotum.*" Milner, in his History of Winchester, *vol.* i. *p.* 42, has strangely denominated Devotus, " a religious *bishop.*" An anonymous writer on Winchester cathedral justly remarks on this subject that, " In attributing the consecration of this cathedral to Romish missionaries, it has been wished to infer that the see of Rome had always spiritual authority over Britain; and that Eleutherius, by this act, obtained the same power over Winchester, which his successors claimed a thousand years after. The very contrary, however, is the fact; and whatever might be the state of religious knowledge in this country during the life of Lucius, even bishop Milner is constrained to admit, that, " it seemed best to him and his prelates [without any reference to the bishop of Rome] that the same hierarchy should be observed which had before obtained among the Flamines, or heathen priests. According to this, London, York, and Caerleon, became metropolitan sees; and hence, *Venta*, although the favourite of Lucius, and probably the capital of his dominions, was left destitute of that pre-eminence to which, as the chief city of the west, it was otherwise entitled."

annexed to it a monastery, whose inmates were of the order of those instituted by St. Mark, at Alexandria[25]. The dimensions of the monastery are stated to have been as follows: " in length, from the eastern part of the church towards the old Temple of Concord, 100 paces; in breadth, towards the new Temple of Apollo, 80 paces: from the north-east part, in length 160 paces, in breadth 98: from the western ground *(plagá)* of the church, in length 190 paces, in breadth 100: from the southern ground, in length 45 paces, in breadth 58 paces."

The striking absurdity of Rudborne, or rather of Moracius, whom he follows, in carrying up the privilege of sanctuary to such an early period[26], could be equalled only by his error in assigning the antiquity of the monastic profession to an era so remote from the true one. Even Milner himself (though sufficiently credulous on many things advanced by this writer) withholds his assent to the latter statement, and declares it to be " not warranted by ecclesiastical monuments[27]."

Rudborne says, that the new church was dedicated in the fifth year of the conversion of the kingdom; or as he afterwards more particularly records it, on the 4th of the kalends of November, in the year of grace 169. His chronology, however, is extremely defective; and by no means to be depended on, unless corroborated by other authorities. The possessions and treasures of the Flamines, he tells us, of this city, were given by Lucius to the bishops and monks of the new foundation[28].

The ambiguity which attends the period of the decease of Lucius, and

[25] Philo, the Jew, calls them *Therapeutes*: *i. e.* a Jewish order of monks devoted to contemplation.

[26] Bingham, in his Orig. Eccles. *vol.* iii. p. 291, says, that " the right of sanctuary began to be a privilege of churches from the time of *Constantine*, though there are no laws about it older than Theodosius, either in the Justinian or the Theodosian Code." There were no monks till after the middle of the third century.

[27] Hist. of Winchester, *vol.* i. *p.* 42, n. In another part he says, that although Rudborne " takes great pains to persuade us that the Winchester monks were of an order anterior to the ages both of St. Benedict and St. Antony, it would be loss of time to confute an account so glaringly improbable." Ib. *vol.* ii. *p.* 3, n.

[28] Rudb. *lib.* i. *c.* 3.

the uncertainty of the place of his burial, have been often adduced as arguments against the credibility of his reputed sway; and it is certain that the darkness in which those circumstances are involved, is calculated to excite considerable suspicion.   Were the accounts true, that Lucius had possessed such extended sovereignty as to occasion the general establishment of Christianity in this island, it is scarcely possible to believe that he could have descended so obscurely to the grave, as to leave the time of his death unascertained, and the place of his interment undecided. Winchester, York, and Gloucester, have all been assigned as the scene of the latter; yet the German writers report, " that a little before his decease, either resigning his crown, or being dispossessed of it by the Romans, he went abroad, and preached the gospel in Bavaria, and in the country of the Grisons[29]." Bishop Godwin refers to R. Vitus, as saying, that "King Lucius, after a certain space forsaking his kingdom, became a clergyman; and preaching the gospel in divers countries of France and Germany, suffered martyrdom, at last, at a place called Curiac[30]."

The dynasty of Lucius is stated to have terminated with his own life, as the Romans afterwards governed directly by their own officers, and not by native tributary princes. The religious establishment, however, which he had fixed at Winchester, is said by Rudborne, to have retained its privileges and continued in repose, till the great persecution carried on against the Christians by the Emperors Dioclesian and Maximian, was extended into Britain, (about the end of the third or beginning of the fourth century), at which period the church and monastery, attributed to Lucius, were levelled with the ground, and all the ecclesiastics either slaughtered or dispersed[31].

The glory of quelling the persecution in this island is ascribed to Constantius Chlorus; whose son and successor, Constantine the Great, by his famous edict in the year 312, restored the Christians to the rights of humanity and civil justice.   The church of Venta was then rebuilt,

[29] Milner's Hist. of Winchester, *vol. i. p.* 43.   [30] Cat. of Eng. Bishops, *p.* 35.

[31] Rudb. *lib.* i. *c.* 4.

according to Rudborne, upon the same site, and in a similar form (that of a cross) to the former one; but on a much smaller scale, the expenses being defrayed by the offerings of the faithful in Christ[32]. When finished it was dedicated, at the request of the Abbot *Deodatus*, by *Constans*, the then bishop, in honour of St. Amphibalus[33], whom the monkish writers record to have suffered martyrdom at Verulam, whither he had sought refuge in the abode of St. Alban, during the Dioclesian persecution; but having been discovered, he was put to death, as was also his kind host for affording him shelter and entertainment.

After the withdrawing of the Roman troops from Britain, on account of the increasing calamities of the Roman Empire, Venta obtained the rank of a metropolis; for here the British King, Vortigern, or Gortheryn, and his successors Ambrosius and Uther Pendragon, fixed their principal residence: yet no particulars are extant of its ecclesiastical history, during this period, than what are afforded by Rudborne, who barely states, that the monks continued to enjoy their privileges in security and peace, " devoutly engaged in singing hymns and holy songs," till the coming of Cerdic, the Saxon chief, and founder of the West-Saxon kingdom. This prince (after defeating the united army of the Britons, under Natanleod, in the New Forest,) besieged and obtained possession of Venta, about the year 516, at which time all the monks were slain, and the Cathedral was converted into a heathen temple[34], and " made subservient to the gloomy

[32] " Reedificata est Ecclesia Wyntoniensis secundo ab Christi fidelium oblationibus." Rudb. *lib.* i. *c.* 6.

[33] Ibid. Rudborne describes St. Amphibalus as " one of the brotherhood" of this church. The Bishop Constans, mentioned in the text, who is said to have been the son of the Emperor Constantine; and who, after the successful usurpation of his father, about the year 407, having been " tempted, or compelled, sacrilegiously to desert the peaceful obscurity of the monastic life," was himself invested with the imperial purple, and left to command in Spain; where, on the revolt of Gerontius, his bravest general, he was made prisoner, and put to death. Vide Gibbon's Decline, &c. of the Roman Empire, *vol.* v. *p.* 342.

[34] Rudb. Hist. *lib.* ii. *c.* 1.—" In loco quem de Christi Ecclesia, *i. e.* Wyntoniensi, Monachis interfectis, Pagani templum fecerant Dagon."

and impure rites of Thor, Woden, Frea, and Tuisco[35]." The name of the city, itself, was also changed, and from Caer-Gwent, and Venta-Belgarum, it became *Winton-ceaster;* and hence Winchester by an easy corruption.

In the year 519, as most of our historians agree, the victorious Cerdic was crowned king of the West Saxons (in conjunction with Kynric, his son) in the church, or temple at Winchester; wherein also, having greatly extended his kingdom by new conquests, and increased his subjects by fresh colonies of Jutes and Saxons, he was again crowned about twelve years afterwards: here, likewise, he was buried, on his decease in 534.

Though the immediate successors of Cerdic considerably extended their dominions, yet they continued to make Winchester their principal seat. No event of particular importance, however, is recorded concerning the Cathedral Church, till after the year 635, when the arrival of the missionary, BIRINUS, whom Pope Honorius had deputed to preach the gospel in those parts of Britain that were still involved in Pagan darkness, entirely changed the state of affairs. This prelate, whose country and origin are dubious, is said to have been a monk at Rome; but, for the purposes of his mission, he was ordained a bishop at Genoa, and thence, proceeding through France, he took shipping for Britain. The sceptre of the West Saxon kingdom was, at that period, swayed by Kinegils and his son Quilchelm; and Birinus, having obtained a favourable reception at the court of those Princes, (through the opportune presence of the religious Oswald, King of the Northumbrians, who was then soliciting the daughter of Kinegils in marriage) commenced his labours in this city. His pious endeavours were quickly rewarded by the conversion of Kinegils and many of his people[36];

[35] From these deities of the Jutes and Saxons, the names are derived of four of our week days. See Verstegan. The Jutes, called also *Giotti* and *Gevissi*, formed the principal tribe that established the West Saxon kingdom.

[36] The sudden influence which Birinus obtained over the minds of the Saxons, is, agreeably to the monkish legends of that age, attributed to the fame of a miracle, which attended his embarkation for this island, and is thus described by Dr. Milner :—

" Proceeding from Genoa, through France, our apostle came to the sea-port on the channel, from which he was to embark for our island. Here, having performed the sacred mysteries, he left behind him what is called a *corporal* [in allusion to the body of Christ] containing the blessed

and it appears from the respective histories of Bede and Malmsbury, that
King Oswald acted in the character of godfather to Kinegils when the
latter was baptized.

Before Birinus quitted Rome, he pledged his word to the Pope, that he
would promulgate Christianity in those parts of Britain where the light of
the gospel had never yet been spread; with this intent, and with the consent
of Kinegils and Oswald, he removed to Dorchester, in Oxfordshire, which
was then a considerable town, and apparently the place were Quilchelm
kept his court[37], as that monarch received baptism there in the following

sacrament, which he did not recollect until the vessel, in which he sailed, was some way out at sea.
It was in vain to argue the case with the Pagan sailors who steered the ship, and it was impossible
for him to leave his treasure behind him. In this extremity, supported by a strong faith, he stepped
out of the ship upon the waters, which became firm under his feet, and walked in this manner to
the land. Having secured what he was anxious about, he returned in the same manner on board
the vessel, which had remained stationary in the place where he had left it. The ship's crew were
of the nation to which he was sent, and being struck with the miracle they had witnessed, lent a
docile ear to his instructions : thus our apostle began the conversion of the West-Saxons before he
landed upon their territory." Hist. of Win. *vol.* i. *p.* 89.

This legend is recorded by several ancient writers, and Dr. Milner regards it as a *prodigy* so
well attested, that those, he says, " who have had the greatest interest to deny it, have *not dared
openly to do so*." The following remark on this passage is extracted from a recent description of
the Cathedral :—" Milner's concluding assertion is singularly bold and fanatical. The persons
alluded to as not daring to deny it, are Bishop Godwin and the truth-telling Fox : the former takes
no notice whatever of this compound miracle, wisely judging it beneath contempt ; and the latter
bestows on it the only correct appellation in our language, that of a lie."

[37] The town of Dorchester is situated near the river Thames, about ten miles south of Oxford.
It was anciently occupied by the Romans, many of whose coins, urns, &c. have been found there,
and considerable entrenchments still remain in the vicinity. The church is a very large and
curious building, and affords numerous vestiges of its former splendour. In the windows are some
remains of ancient painted glass, which some years ago were collected from different parts of the
edifice, and put up in the chancel : among the subjects that continue whole is a full length
figure of St. Birinus, as well as several small compartments relating to his history. The windows
in the chancel are very curious and singular : that on the north side is large and lofty, divided into
four days by three mullions, which internally assume the form of branches of trees. This is
intended to represent the genealogical tree of Jesse, whose figure is prostrate at the bottom, and
several smaller statues are displayed in other parts of the tree. Among the tombs is a fine
effigy of a *Crusader*, in mail armour; and also the figure of another armed knight, well executed,

year (anno 636): three years afterwards Cuthred, his son, was baptized in the same city, Birinus himself being his sponsor.

From this era the ecclesiastical history of Winchester becomes more certain, as the concurring testimony of different historians substantiate the leading facts; for whatever has been affirmed on the authority of Rudborne, as to the existence of a Bishopric in this city, prior to the Saxon times, is extremely doubtful; the historians most to be depended on being unanimous in ascribing the foundation both of the See and the Cathedral to Kenewalsh, the son and successor of Kinegils.

Though Birinus had established his episcopal seat at Dorchester, (which had been given to him by Kinegils), yet that appears to have been done provisionally, only " till a church were built in the royal city, worthy of such a priest[38]." For this purpose Kinegils collected a great quantity of materials; and he intended, according to the Winchester Annalist, to bestow on the new foundation all the land round this city, to the extent of seven leagues[39]. Being seized, however, with a mortal illness before he had completed his design, he caused his son Kenewalsh to swear, in the presence of Birinus, " that he would punctually fulfil these his pious intentions." This was in the year 643; when dying, his remains were interred within the pale of the new church, of which he had begun the foundation[40].

but much broken. There is, likewise, the effigy of a bishop, *in pontificalibus*, and two stone coffins; the latter were dug up, the one about seven, the other about twelve years ago, in the south aile, within eighteen inches of the surface; each of these is formed out of a single stone. Several other churches are said to have formerly stood in this town; and many human bones and vestiges of antient sepulture are occasionally met with in digging in various parts of the neighbourhood. The site of the ancient Episcopal Palace is still pointed out in the appurtenances to a farm-house closely adjacent to the town.

[38] " Iste dedit S. Birino Civitatem Dorcacestram; ut sederet interim in eâ, donec conderet Ecclesiam tanto sacerdote dignam in regiâ civitate."—Ann. Eccl. Winton. in Ang. Sacra. *vol*. 1, 128.

[39] " In votis enim ejus [Kinegils] erat in Wintoniâ ædificare templum præcipuum; et collectis jam plurimis ad opus ædificii, terram totam ambientem Wintoniam à centro Wintoniæ usque ad circumferentiam ab omni parte lineâ exeunte septem leucas habentem ædificandæ Ecclesiæ in dotem dare disposuit.—Ann. Eccl. Winton. ibid.

[40] " —et in Wyntoniâ, quam fundare incœperat, honorificè sepelitur."—Rudb. *lib*. ii. *c*. 1. ibid. 189.

D

Kenewalsh was a Pagan, and during several years he neglected the execution of his oath ; but having been dispossessed of his throne by Penda, King of Mercia, (whose daughter he had married, and afterwards repudiated,) he became a convert to Christianity, at the court of Anna, the pious King of the East Angles, to which he had fled for an asylum. Being afterwards restored to his kingdom, through the interposition of his friends, and particularly of his kinsman, Cuthred, he proceeded with the building of the Cathedral, and completed it about the year 648, in a style of considerable splendour for that age[41]. It was then dedicated by St. Birinus, as he is styled in the Roman Calendar, in honour of the Holy Trinity, and of St. Peter and St. Paul; and the conventual buildings, which had been also restored by Kenewalsh, were replenished either with secular or regular canons, but most probably the former ; as the unnatural celibacy of the Romish clergy had not, at that period, obtained such a pre-dominance in this country, as it subsequently did, under the tyrannic sway of the famous St. Dunstan. Birinus afterwards returned to Dorchester, where he died, and was buried, in the year 640 ; but his remains were translated to Winchester by Bishop Hedda, on the final removal of the see to the latter city.

AGILBERT, or ANGILBERT, a native of France, who had long studied in Ireland, (which at that period seems to have been eminently distinguished for its schools and literature), was prevailed on by Kenewalsh to succeed Birinus, with whom he had been previously associated in promulgating the gospel. The foreign accents of this prelate, however, proved disagreeable to the Saxon King ; and the latter, about the year 660, divided the diocess into two portions ; assigning to the see of Dorchester the jurisdiction over the northern part of Wessex, and establishing Winchester as the see of the southern part. This era, therefore, strictly speaking, must be considered as that of the foundation of the Bishopric of Winchester.

---

[41] " —Templum Deo, per id temporis, pulcherrimum, construeret,"—are the words of William of Malmsbury. " De Gest. Reg." *l*. 1, *c.* 2. Rudborne says, " Ecclesiam pulcherrimam construxit in Wyntoniâ." " Ann. Eccl. Winton." *p.* 288.

Agilbert, says Bishop Godwin, " taking this matter very grievously (the rather because it was done altogether without either his consent or knowledge) returned in a great chafe into his own country, where soon after he was made bishop of Paris[42]." Through this abandonment of his duties, the direction of both sees became vested in WINA, an Englishman of great talents, whom Kenewalsh had raised to the episcopal seat at Winchester, but who, three years afterwards, was again expelled by that King; though from what cause historians have neglected to record[43]. Both sees were now kept vacant four years; when Kenewalsh, becoming alarmed by some defeats in battle and other adversities, (which he attributed to his late neglect of religion,) dispatched an embassy to request Agilbert to return to his former diocess. This, Agilbert declined, but recommended his nephew ELEUTHE-RIUS as a fit person to be appointed in his stead. He was accordingly received with much welcome both by the prince and people, and in the year 670 was consecrated bishop over the entire diocess, by Theodore, Archbishop of Canterbury. He chiefly resided in Winchester, and is recorded to have been very sedulous in the discharge of his duties. Amongst other pious works, he assisted St. Aldhelm in raising the hermitage of Maidulph, an Irish nobleman, into the famous Abbey of Malmsbury; which afterwards became so deservedly celebrated as the principal school and seat of learning in the west of England. He died in 674, and was buried in this Church; in which, also about the same period, King Kenewalsh himself was interred; he having previously endowed the new establishment with all the lands designed by his father for that purpose, together with the manors of Downton, Alresford, and Worthy[44]. His kinsman, Escuin, or Escwine, who had been raised to the throne on the expulsion of Sexburga (Kenewalsh's widow) died about the year 676, and

---

[42] Cat. of Eng. Bishops, *p.* 210.

[43] Wina, after his expulsion, took refuge in Mercia; of whose sovereign, Wulfhere, or Wulphere, he is said to have *purchased* the bishopric of London, about the year 666; he " being the first Simonist," says Godwin, that is mentioned in our country.

[44] Ann. Winton. anno 639.

was deposited here with his predecessors; as was likewise his successor, Kentwin, (a son to Kinegils), who died in 685.

After the death of Bishop Eleutherius, the vacant see was bestowed on HEDDA, Abbot of Streneschal, or Whitby, in Yorkshire; whom Bede testifies to have been rather a good and just man than profoundly learned. By him the seat of the diocess was formally translated from Dorchester, about the year 676, and settled at Winchester; whither also, he removed the sainted remains of Birinus. Hedda, dying about the year 705, was interred in this Cathedral: Bede reports that many miracles were wrought at his tomb, the fame of which appears to have led to his canonization by the Romish Church.

At the period of Hedda's decease, the West Saxon kingdom had been greatly enlarged by new conquests; and the knowledge of Christianity having, in consequence, been more extensively promulgated, it became necessary again to divide the diocess into two distinct sees. This act of jurisdiction, according to Godwin[45], was executed by the sole authority of the famous King Ina; yet William of Malmsbury states it to have been done by an Episcopal Synod[46]. The new See was fixed at Sherborne, in Dorsetshire, and had assigned to it the counties of Berks, Dorset, Somerset, Wilts, Devon, and Cornwall. The See of Winchester retained the counties of Hants, Surrey, Sussex, and the Isle of Wight. The learned St. Aldhelm, Abbot of Malmsbury, was then made Bishop of Sherborne; and DANIEL, a monk of the same foundation, and also a renowned scholar, was raised to the Bishopric of Winchester. In his time (anno 711) another division of this diocess was effected by the erection of Sussex into an Episcopal province, and fixing its See at the monastery of Selsea, or Seolsey; which seat was subsequently removed to Chichester. A few years afterwards King Ina, influenced by religious zeal, resigned his crown, and with his pious Queen, Ethelburga, proceeded to Rome in disguise, having previously

---

[45] De Præsul. p. 205.

[46] " Synodali ergo concilio diocesis, ultra modum protensa, in duas sedes divisa." Malm. in Vit. St. Aldhelm, Ang. Sac. vol. ii. p. 20.

refounded the Abbey of Glastonbury, and given eighty hides of land, in the Isle of Wight, to this church[47]. Athelard, Ina's nephew and successor, died in 741, and was interred at Winchester, together with his sister, Frideswitha.

In the year 744, Bishop Daniel, who had presided over this see during upwards of forty years, relinquished his charge through the infirmities of age; and re-assuming the habit of a monk, retired to his original solitude at Malmsbury, where he ended his days. Venerable Bede, in the Preface to his Ecclesiastical History, has acknowledged his literary obligations to this prelate; who, besides some other works, was the writer of a life of St. Chad, and of Histories of the South Saxons and the Isle of Wight.

During the supremacy of the eight succeeding bishops, namely, HUMFRED, KINEBARD, ATHELARD (who had been Abbot of Malmsbury, and was translated from Winchester to Canterbury in 793), EGBALD, DUDDA, or *Dudd*, KINEBERT, or *Cinebord*, ALMUND, and WIGHTEN, no event of particular importance occurred relating to this church, with the exception of the burials here of the West Saxon Kings, Cuthred, Sigebert, and Kynewulph; and the memorable coronation of King EGBERT, in the year 827. This prince, who in the early part of his life had been banished by King Brithric, had so diligently studied the example of the great Charlemagne, as to become his rival on this side of the water, when called to the West Saxon throne, on the death of Brithric, in 800. After many severe battles, he obtained the ascendancy over all the other Saxon states, and, uniting the whole into one Monarchy, caused himself to be solemnly crowned *King of all Britain* in Winchester Cathedral, and in presence of the assembled nobles from every part of the country. On this occasion, by an edict dated from this city, he formally abolished all distinctions of Saxons, Jutes, and *English*; commanding that all his subjects should in future be called by the latter name only, and the country be called England.

---

[47] Ina died at Rome, in the year 728, according to the Saxon Chronicle; but his Queen, having returned to England, retired to the Abbey of Barking, in Essex, (of which her sister was abbess) and died there in 741.

Bishop Wighten, who is supposed to have had the honour of crowning Egbert, died within two or three years after that event, and was succeeded by HEREFRITH; of whom nothing more is recorded than the circumstance of his being slain in the year 833, together with Wigforth, Bishop of Sherborne, in the disastrous battle of Charmouth, in Dorsetshire, whither these prelates had attended the King to oppose the Danes, who had landed on that coast in great force. EADMUND, or *Edmund*, the next bishop, governed the diocess only a few months; when, dying, he was succeeded by the venerable HELMSTAN, or *Helinstan*, (as he is styled by Rudborne), who was a canon of this church, and had been entrusted with the education of Egbert's son, Ethelwulph. This young Prince is thought to have been intended for a religious life, and it is certain that both his inclinations and his talents were far better adapted for the direction of a church than the government of a kingdom. His more immediate tutor was the famous SWITHUN, or *Swithin*, (as the name has been spelt in modern times;) " the opinion of whose holiness," says Godwin, " hath procured him the reputation of a Saint." Under this preceptor he became, first, a canon, and afterwards sub-dean of this Cathedral; and he seems to have held the latter situation when advanced to the throne on the decease of King Egbert, in 837[48]. Several ancient writers state, that the demise of Bishop Helmstan occurred about the same period, and that Ethelwulph was himself raised to the vacant see; yet the probability is, that he was never actually consecrated, though he might have been elected to the episcopal dignity. However this may be, it appears that the prince, being in holy orders in this monastery, had a dispensation from Pope Leo the Third to enable him to assume the crown.

Rudborne says, that Helmstan being dead, Ethelwulph, in the fifteenth year of his reign, and in the year 852, ordered the most pious Swithun to be preferred to this see[49]; yet it would seem from other historians, that

---

[48] — patre defuncto, quia alius legitimus hæres non extaret, exgradu Subdiaconi Wintoniensis in Regem translatus est, concedente Leone illius nominis Papa tertio. Will. Malm. De Pontif. *l.* ii. in Rer. Ang Scrip. *p.* 242. Vide also, Joan. Wallingford, in Chron. Ranulph. Higden. Ad. An. 836. Rudb. Hist. Maj. *l.* iii. *c.* 2. [49] Vide Hist. Maj. *l.* iii. *c.* 2.

Swithun must have been appointed bishop here many years before. This famed prelate was a native either of the city or suburbs of Winchester; and, early in life, he became a canon of this Church. He was highly distinguished for his piety and knowledge of sacred literature; and William of Malmsbury styles him a " treasury of virtues," the most conspicuous of which were his meekness and humility. The influence which he had obtained over the youthful mind of Ethelwulph, he continued to possess in the maturer age of that prince; and it is recorded to have been by his advice, that Ethelwulph, in a " Mycel Synod," granted his famous charter for the general establishment of tythes, in the year 854 or 855[50]. This important deed was executed at Winchester, as appears from the charter itself, as copied in the histories of Matthew of Westminster, Ingulphus, Rudborne, and other writers. " The instrument testifies, that it was subscribed by Ethelwulph himself, and by his two vassals, Burred, King of Mercia, and Edmund, King of the East Angles; as also by a great number of nobles, prelates, &c. in the Cathedral Church at Winchester, before the high altar; and that, being thus signed, it was, by way of greater solemnity, placed by the King upon the altar[51]." Ethelwulph died in 857, and was buried near Egbert, his father, in this Church; the possessions of which had been much augmented by these princes.

Through the counsels of Swithun, King Ethelbald, (Ethelwulph's successor,) raised *fortifications* round the Cathedral and cloisters, in order to protect them from the destructive fury of the Danes, who had now begun to make frequent incursions into different parts of the kingdom, with large armies. The good effects of this measure were soon experienced, for in the next reign, that of Ethelbert, the Danes landed a considerable force at Southampton, and advancing to Winchester, made themselves masters of the city, wherein they committed the most barbarous and lamentable

[50] Malm. De Gest. Reg.   Butler's " Lives of the Fathers," &c. *vol.* iv. *p.* 196.

[51] Miln. Hist. of Win. *vol.* i. *p.* 120, 121.   Besides the charter mentioned above, there is another extant to the same effect, which Ethelwulph is said to have granted in the year 854, at the feast of Easter, and is dated at the Palace of Wilton.   The latter charter is given in Dugdale's Monasticon, but it is generally considered to be spurious.

excesses; but the Cathedral, with its adjoining offices, appear to have escaped their rage, a circumstance only to be accounted for by supposing the whole to have been completely secured from their depredations. The Danes, on retreating to their ships, were routed with great slaughter, by the Earls of Hampshire and Berkshire; and the immense spoils which they had made in this city were recovered. These events appear to have taken place about 860; two or three years after which St. Swithun died, and agreeably to his own desire, was interred here, in the church-yard. He is said to have been an especial benefactor to Winchester, and to have either originally constructed, or rebuilt, the principal city-bridge[52]. He has the praise likewise of building a number of churches in those parishes where none had before existed: the monkish annalists, however, not being content with the renown really due to his sanctity and merits, have attributed to him various miracles. Godwin says, that " his learning questionless was great[53];" and Rudborne affirms, that Ethelwulph's youngest son, Alfred, whose immortal actions have procured him the surname of *Great*, was in his very infancy committed to the care and tuition of this prelate[54].

ALFRITH, or *Adferth*, the next bishop, a man of great learning, governed this see " discreetly and wisely" about eleven years, after which he appears to have been translated to Canterbury, and is distinguished in the annals of that city by the name of *Athelred*.   His successor was

---

[52] Warton, in his History of English Poetry, *vol.* i. *p.* 15, has quoted the following passage from a very ancient versification of the Lives of the Saints:—

> Seynt Swythan his bushopricke to al goodnesse brough :
> The towne also of Wynchestre he amended inough.
> Ffor he lette the stronge bruge, without the toune arere,
> And fond thereto lym and ston and the workmen that ther were.

[53] Cat. of Eng. Bish. *p.* 213. " How miraculously he made whole a basket of egges that were all broken, and some other thinges accounted miracles in our histories, who so list may reade in Matthew Westminster, in his report of the yeere 862, at what time, July 2, this bishop died." Ib. William of Malmsbury states that he died in 863.

[54] Hist. Maj. *l.* 3, *c.* vi.

DUNBERT, who is recorded to have settled certain lands upon this Cathedral, for its repairs, which measure had become necessary through the devastations committed here by the Danes; who, after several desperate battles with the Princes Ethelred and Alfred, had penetrated to Winchester, where, obtaining possession of the Church, they massacred every individual belonging to it that fell into their power[55].

On the death of Ethelred, who had been mortally wounded in battle, in the year 872, his brother Alfred was crowned king, in Winchester Cathedral; but after a perturbed sway of several years, he was, at length, forced by the Danes to seek an asylum in the abode of a swine-herd, or neat-herd, in the Isle of Athelney, in Somersetshire; amidst the almost impassible marshes formed by the conflux of the Perrot and the Thone. After an inglorious obscurity of some months, he suddenly emerged from this retreat, and with a united band of faithful partizans (which had been privately assembled on the eastern borders of Selwood Forest) he surprised and defeated the Danish army at *Ethandune*, or Heddington, in Wiltshire[56]. This victory led the way to new achievements, and Alfred's subsequent successes restored to him his capital and kingdom. Hence Winchester again became the seat of government, and its Cathedral establishment was once more replenished with secular canons.

Bishop Dunbert died in the year 879, and was succeeded by DENEWULF, or *Denulf;* of whom ancient writers report, that he was the very herdsman in whose cottage and service Alfred had been concealed at Athelney. Godwin says, that the king " having recovered the peaceable possession of his crown, was not unmindful of his old master, in whom perceiving an excellent sharpness of wit, he caused him (though it were now late, he being a man growne) to study, and having obtained some competency in learning, he preferred him to the bishopricke of Winchester[57]." He proved

[55] Rudborne places this event in 866; but the more probable date is the year 871, as assigned by Wharton, in Aug. Sac. *vol.* i. *p.* 206, n.

[56] Heddington is about six miles south of Chippenham. See an account of this battle, with observations on its supposed site, in my account of Wiltshire: Beauties of England, *vol.* xv., also Whitaker's " Life of St. Neot."   [57] Cat. of Eng. Bish. *p.* 215.

E

an active and able prelate; and, as appears from the researches of the learned Spelman, was one of the king's chief counsellors[58].

The Great Alfred, in his latter years, began the foundation of a magnificent abbey in the Cathedral Cemetery at Winchester, for the purpose of retaining in England his friend and chaplain, Grimbald; who had been originally a monk at St. Bertin's monastery, in Artois, and had been invited into England by the king, to assist in establishing an University. Whitaker, in his 'Life of St. Neot,' contends that the first English University, or public school, was founded at Winchester, and not at Oxford, as generally asserted and believed. Alfred also intended the new abbey as a burial place for himself and his family; but dying before its completion (in 900 or 901), he was provisionally interred in the Cathedral, under a monument of porphyry marble, from which his remains were afterwards translated to the *Newen-Mynstre*, as his foundation was then termed.

Denewulf, according to Matthew of Westminster, was succeeded by Bishop ATHELM; who, in the year 888, travelled to Rome with the alms collected by King Alfred and Archbishop Plegmund. His successor, as appears from the same writer, was BERTULF; whom Alfred, in the year 897, appointed one of the guardians of the realm, to defend it against the Danes[59]. Neither of these prelates are named by Rudborne; who, on the contrary, states, that Denewulf held this see twenty-four years; and that Edward the Elder exchanged with him a certain quantity of land, for that of the cemetery and other ground belonging to the Cathedral, on which the new monastery was built[60]. If this account be true, there is evidently no time for the succession of Athelm and Bertulf; as Denewulf's decease, (when calculated from the date of that of Dunbert his predecessor) could not have happened till the year 903.

The chronological difficulties which attend the ecclesiastical history of Winchester about this era, are probably inexplicable[61]; and they have been the more involved through the endeavours of the Roman Catholic writers to trace the direct supremacy of the Papal See over the English Church to

[58] In Vit. Alfr. *p.* 102.

[59] Vide Godwin. De Presul. under Winchester.

[60] Rudb. Hist. Maj. *l.* iii. *c.* 7.

[61] Vide Wharton's Angl. Sac. *vol.* i. *p.* 209, n.

the period now mentioned.   It is stated by Malmsbury[62], under the date 904, that Pope Formosus having been informed that the West Saxon sees had remained vacant during the space of seven years, sent a Bull into England, excommunicating the King and all his subjects, on account of this irregularity ; and that, in consequence, the King (who must have been Edward the Elder) caused Plegmund, Archbishop of Canterbury, to assemble, at Winchester, a general Council, or Synod, (of bishops, abbots, and other dignified persons,) in which it was determined that the vacancies should not only be filled, but that three new Sees should be established in the West Saxon states.   The archbishop, who had presided at the meeting, is then said to have proceeded to Rome, to get the censure taken off, and on his return home, to have consecrated seven new bishops in one day.   The year generally assigned for this remarkable consecration is 905 ; but Sir H. Spelman and Johnson refer it to 908.

Against the presumed authenticity of the above Bull, it has been fatally objected, that Pope Formosus died in 895, or 896 ; and therefore could never have signed such an instrument in 904.   To solve this difficulty, Baronius conceives that Malmsbury's date is wrong, and should have been 894 ; yet if this were the fact, the sovereign excommunicated must have been Alfred ; yet no historian has ever glanced at such an event in respect to that monarch.   Other difficulties, equally insuperable, attend this conjecture. Johnson, in " Ecclesiastical Laws," &c. refers this Bull to Pope Sergius, by which means, he says, " all runs clear."   " We cannot wonder," he says, " if the monks chose to report this papal act as done by Formosus, who was a popular Pope, and made more popular by the barbarous treatment of his dead corpse and memory, than by such a monster of a man and Pope, as Sergius."

That the West Saxon demesne was divided into several distinct Sees about this time ; and that seven Bishops were actually consecrated on one day by Plegmund, are circumstances so positively affirmed by various historians, that their validity cannot consistently be questioned.   Three of the new Sees were taken from the diocess of Sherborne, and were fixed at Wells, for Somersetshire ; at Crediton, or Kyrton, for Devonshire ; and at

[62] Malm. De Gest. Reg. l. ii.

Petrock's-Stow, for Cornwall: by this arrangement Dorsetshire, Wiltshire, and Berkshire, were the only counties that remained subordinate to Sherborne. The diocess of Winchester was left to its former limits; but among the seven Bishops (all of whom were consecrated at Canterbury,) we find that one, named Kenulf, or Ceolwulph, was appointed for the ancient See of Dorchester, in Oxfordshire[63].

The prelate now chosen to preside over this diocess, was FRITHSTAN, who had been a scholar of St. Grimbald, and a canon in the New Minster in this city. He was much renowned for his piety and learning, and having governed this See, in an exemplary manner, about twenty-two years, he resigned his bishopric to BRINSTAN, or *Birnstan*, (whom he had previously consecrated), and after passing the remainder of his days in devotional exercises, died in 932. Brinstan was originally one of the secular clergy belonging to the Cathedral, but he afterwards assumed the cowl in St. Grimbald's new abbey: his most prominent virtues were charity and humility; and he was accustomed to walk round the church-yards by night, praying for the dead[64]: he died on the feast of All Souls, 934, whilst in the act of prayer, in his oratory. In the following year he was succeeded by ELPHEGE *the First*, surnamed the Bald, who had been a monk of Glastonbury, and was uncle to the famous St. Dunstan, whom he raised to the order of priesthood in this Cathedral. He is said to have excelled in all the Christian virtues, and to have bequeathed his lands to certain churches and monasteries in Winchester; subject, however, to the payment of some annuities to relations: he died in the year 951. " Of these three bishops," says Godwin, " divers miracles are reported in histories, which need not be here rehearsed." They were all buried in this Church, and are all ranked as saints in the Roman Calendar.

ELSIN, or *Alfin*, the next bishop, was a man of royal blood, and of extraordinary learning; but he has had the misfortune to be greatly calum-

[63] Will. Malm. Rudb. Matt. West. Rapin says, that " though Malmsbury and Higden affirm the new-erected Bishopricks had the Pope's confirmation, it is certain at that time, and for more than 200 years after, there was no such thing required." Hist. of Eng. *vol. i. p.* 113.

[64] One night, on finishing his devotions among the tombs, (in the cemetery of St. Anastasius), his ' *Requiescant in pace*' is recorded to have been loudly answered by an infinite multitude of voices from the sepulchre, ejaculating ' *Amen* ' Vide Rudb. Hist. Maj. *l.* iii. *e.* 8.

niated through aiding King Edwy to repress the tyranny and insolence of the monks[65]. In his time, anno 955, the remains of Edwy's predecessor, Edgar, were interred in Winchester Cathedral, with great solemnity, by Dunstan; who having been sent for to administer the sacrament to the expiring King, came not till too late : yet he had the hardihood to testify, that, on his journey, he had been assured by a celestial voice of the happiness of the deceased sovereign[66]!

On the decease of Archbishop Odo, in 958, Elsin was translated to the See of Canterbury, to which he appears to have been nominated by the King, from his affinity to the blood-royal ; though his enemies state that he obtained his election by bribery and corrupt intrigues. The manner of his

[65] The coronation of Edwy (a youth of fourteen) at Winchester, was attended by some remarkable events, which in their consequences, are thought to have had great influence over the affairs of this church. The generality of the monkish historians concur in representing that Edwy had been corrupted by a lascivious female of high birth and great beauty, named Algiva, who had a daughter equally shameless; and that he withdrew from the company of his nobles, at the coronation feast, in order to solace himself in their lewd society. The guests, indignant at this treatment, ordered his tutor, Dunstan (who was then Abbot of Glastonbury), and Kinsey, Bishop of Lichfield, to conduct the youth back to the assembly; and Dunstan had the boldness to reprimand him for thus inconsiderately giving way to his passions. Edwy was highly exasperated at being thus reproved, and, being yet more irritated by Dunstan's general arrogance, he deprived that ambitious prelate of all his preferments, and forced him into exile. Still further to divest him of his influence, he expelled all the monks of his order from their several monasteries, and replaced them by secular clergy. This procedure, however, proved the ruin of Edwy; for the clamours of the monks were so great, that a successful rebellion was excited against him, and more than half his kingdom submitted to the sway of Edgar, his brother; who immediately recalled Dunstan from banishment, and made him Bishop of Worcester. Edwy died in 959; and Edgar having succeeded to the entire possession of the monarchy, promoted Dunstan to the Archiepiscopal See of Canterbury. The historian of Ramsey Abbey mentions nothing of the coronation feast, but traces Edwy's aversion to the monks to his having been offended by St. Dunstan, and Archbishop Odo; who had obliged him " to repudiate a certain young and beauteous kinswoman of his, with whom he had contracted an illicit marriage." Hist. Ramesiensis, *l. i. c.* 7.

[66] This tale is related by most of the monkish writers; yet they add also, as if to make it the more ludicrously absurd, that Dunstan's *horse,* " trembling at the thunder of the angelic voice," fell dead under him, "astounded at the prodigious noise." Vide Rudb. Hist. Maj. *l.* iii. *c.* 10. Will. Malm. Rog. Hoveden. Mat. West. Osborn. Hist. Ram. *l.* i. *c.* 7.

death was remarkable, for, " being impatient to procure the papal confirmation and pall, he hastened to Rome in the most unseasonable weather;
when, in crossing the Alps, he experienced such intense cold, as induced
him to cause the bodies of the horses, on which he and his companions
rode, to be cut open, in order to preserve his own vital heat, by plunging
his feet into them ; but this expedient failing, he died amidst the snow[67]."
His body was brought to England and deposited in this Church; in the
government of which he had been succeeded by BRITHELM, of whom
nothing more is recorded, than that he held the See about five years, and
died in 963.

The next bishop was the famous ST. ETHELWOLD, a native of Winchester,
and of respectable parentage. He commenced his studies, and entered
into holy orders, in this city ; but afterwards became a monk and dean of
Glastonbury, under Dunstan, by whose influence with King Edred he was
made Abbot of the newly-restored monastery of Abingdon, in Berkshire.
Hence, according to Milner, " he was forcibly withdrawn, for the purpose
of undertaking the pastoral government of this, his native city;" but the
rather, as appeared by his actions, with the view of aiding Dunstan (who
was now seated in the archiepiscopal chair at Canterbury) in the accom-
plishment of his long-cherished design of establishing a general celibacy
of the clergy. To effect this, all the secular canons, who refused to
repudiate their wives, and conform to the observances of the Benedictine
Order, were expelled from the Cathedrals and larger Monasteries, under a
commission granted by King Edgar. In the very year of his consecration,
Ethelwold forcibly ejected the secular clergy of this Church, who, among
other vices, of which they were accused, are represented as gluttons,
drunkards, and adulterers[66]. This expulsion was effected with all the

[67] Milner's Winchester, *vol.* i. *p.* 139, from William of Malmsbury. Rudborne, &c. These
writers state, that some such fearful vengeance had been foretold to him, in a vision, by Odo; in
consequence of his having despitefully spurned at the tomb of that prelate in Canterbury Cathedral.

[66] This alleged depravity is said to have been a consequence, partly, of the early licentiousness
and irreligion of King Edwy, (as alluded to in note 65), and partly, of there having been such a
prelate as Elsin seated in the episcopal chair. Vide Miln. Hist. *vol.* i. *p.* 165.

promptitude of determined authority. " He ordered," says Milner, from the old historians, " a proper number of cowls to be brought into the choir, in the midst of the canons; and after a pathetic discourse on the sanctity of their state of life, he left it to their choice, either to put on those religious habits, and embrace the monastic state, or quit the service of the Cathedral. Three of the number were content to enter on this strict course of life; the rest gave up their stalls in the choir, which were soon after filled by a colony of [Benedictine] monks from Abingdon[69]." In the following year he also expelled the canons of the New Minster, who are said to have been even more hardened in wickedness than those of the Cathedral[70].

On the accession of Edward, surnamed the Martyr, (anno 975) Elfrida, his step-mother, attempted to counteract Dunstan's influence, and is said to have caused three abbies, which Ethelwold had founded, to be suppressed, and their possessions to be given to married clergymen[71]. This, and other opposition to his grand designs, occasioned Dunstan to assemble a Synod in the refectory of the Cathedral monastery in this city, in which it was debated whether the regular, or the secular, foundations,

[69] History of Winchester, *vol.* i. *p. 166.*

[70] The monks aver that some of the displaced canons, not brooking the disgrace they had sustained, carried their resentment so far as to attempt to poison St. Ethelwold; but that the saint, though suffering excruciating torment in consequence of swallowing the potion they had prepared for him, was suddenly restored to health, through his prayers to God, and confidence in Christ's promises.

[71] Elfrida's conduct, in this instance, is stated to have arisen from being defeated in her design of raising her own son, Ethelbert, to the throne (in place of Edward) by the firmness of the Saints Dunstan, Oswald, and Ethelwold. How highly those personages were estimated by the monks, may be seen from the following passage:—

' These three brilliant lights, namely, *Dunstan, Oswald,* and *Æthelwold,* by the three candlesticks placed at Canterbury, Worcester, and Winchester, (the Lord so disposing it) irradiated the three parts of the English world with such a brightness, shining from the true Light, that they seemed to contend with even the very stars of the firmament; and were deservedly (by some men living) accounted to be formed by a miracle, through the unusual pre-eminence of so great a sanctity.' Hist. Ram. *c.* xiii. In Decem. Scrip.

should be dissolved. From the opinions of the majority, it seemed probable that the question would have been decided against the monks; but a voice, said to be supernatural, issuing from a crucifix, which hung aloft in the room, is recorded to have determined it in their favour[72]! In that age, indeed, miracles abounded, particularly in respect to Dunstan; whom the monkish writers represent as being so peculiarly favoured by heaven, that there was scarcely an event of his life, of any importance, but what was accompanied by some prodigy.

Ethelwold, leaving his conduct to the secular clergy out of consideration, appears to have been a munificent and charitable prelate. He either founded or rebuilt the several churches and monasteries of Ely, Peterborough, and Thorney; besides assisting in other monastic establishments. His grand undertaking, however, was the rebuilding of his own Cathedral Church, (which was now, for the first time, furnished with a crypt, or crypts, under the east end[73]), and on its completion, in 980, he re-consecrated it with great solemnity, in the presence of King Ethelred, Archbishop Dunstan, and eight bishops, besides a numerous assemblage of nobles and gentry. On this occasion, to its former patrons St. Peter and St. Paul, was added the name of St. Swithun, whose remains had been previously removed from the church-yard, and re-interred under a magnificent shrine that had been provided for the purpose by King Edgar. The fame of the many miracles wrought by St. Swithun's intercession, was the cause of his relics being thus honoured[74]; and hence-forward, till the period of the Dissolution, this establishment was distinguished by the name of St. Swithun's Church and Priory.

Among Ethelwold's public charities it is recorded, to his immortal honour, that in the time of a great famine, he brake all the plate of his Church, and gave it to the poor; saying, that " the Church might be again provided with necessary ornaments, but that if the poor were starved, they could not be

[72] Vide Will. Malm. *l.* ii. *c.* 9. Osborn. Rudb. &c.

[73] " In super occultis studuisti et addere cryptas." Wolstan. Ep. ad. S. Elph.

[74] Will. Malm. De Pontif.

recovered." This prelate died in 984, and was interred in the southern crypt of his own Church[75].

St. Elphege the Second, surnamed the Martyr, was in the same year consecrated to this See, by Dunstan; his austerities and extraordinary abstinence, which, in those days, were considered as proofs of superior sanctity, having recommended him to the Archbishop as a fit person to succeed Ethelwold. He was born of a noble family, and in early youth became a monk at Deerhurst, in Gloucestershire. He was afterwards Prior of Glastonbury, " which place, after a season," says Godwin, " he left, and gave himself to a very strait kind of life at Bath, for which he was so much admired, (the rather because he was a gentleman of great lineage) that many went about to imitate him, and joining themselves to him, made him their governor, by the name of an Abbot[76]." He was thence promoted to this See, which he governed in an exemplary manner during twenty-two years: he was particularly attentive to the poor; and is recorded to have first introduced the use of *Organs* into his Cathedral. In the year 1006, he was raised to the Archbishopric of Canterbury, which he continued to possess till 1013, when he was barbarously massacred by the Danes, at Greenwich, in Kent, after a captivity of seven months. Hence, and from his devotional exercises, and extraordinary and unnatural abstemiousness, (which Osbern says had reduced his body to a seeming skeleton[77]), he is ranked, in the Roman Calendar, both as a saint and a martyr.

Kenulph, or *Elsius*, Abbot of Peterborough, was made Bishop of Winchester on the translation of Elphege to Canterbury. Godwin says he was

---

[75] Capgrave states, that the episcopal Chair of St. Ethelwold long remained an object of popular veneration; it being believed, that if those who sat in it gave way to sloth and drowsiness, they were punished by terrific visions and painful sensations!

[76] Cat. of English Bishops, *p.* 66. Elphege's place of retirement at Bath had been previously a monastery founded by King Offa, about 775, but afterwards destroyed by the Danes. John de Villule, a French physician, who had been made Bishop of Wells, purchased Bath of William Rufus, for 500 marks, and subsequently transferred thither his Episcopal See; for the reception of which he rebuilt the Abbey which Elphege had founded, and which, with great part of the city, had been destroyed by fire. Ib. *p.* 362.

[77] In Vit. Will Malm.

F

" a man infamous for simony and aspiring by corrupt means to this place;" which he enjoyed but little more than one year, being " called by death from his dear-bought preferment[78]." He was interred in this Church; as was likewise his successor BRITHWOLD, or *Ethelwold*, who governed this See till his decease in 1015[79]. He was succeeded by ELSIN, or *Alsin*; whom Godwin has erroneously stated to have been exalted to Canterbury in 1038, but whom most of the ancient historians affirm to have died in 1032[80]: he also was buried in this Cathedral.

ALWYN, a Norman by birth, and kinsman to Queen Emma, was next raised to this bishopric, through the Queen's influence with Canute, her second husband; who, on the decease of Edmund Ironside, about two years before, had obtained the entire sovereignty of the kingdom, and fixed his capital in this city. Emma, " the pearl of Normandy," was daughter to Duke Richard, who appointed Alwyn to accompany her to England in quality of counsellor, or guardian; previously to her first marriage with Ethelred-the-Unready. Alwyn continued at the English court, and whilst yet a layman, was made Earl of Southampton, and invested with a command against the Danes; but after the peace between Edmund and Canute had left him at liberty to pursue his own inclinations for a religious life, he became a monk of Winchester about the year 1016. He was soon afterwards raised to the office of sacristan; a circumstance that has been supposed to account for the profusion of rich gifts bestowed on this Cathedral by King Canute. Besides a large and costly shrine for containing the remains of St. Birinus, that sovereign presented the church with a prodigious chandelier, of solid silver, various ensigns, and other costly ornaments of plate and jewels; but the most extraordinary of all his gifts was that of his royal crown, (which he ordered to be placed over the crucifix of the high altar) having vowed never more to wear such an emblem of authority, from the time that, when seated on the beach, near Southampton, he proved to his attendants, by commanding in vain *the*

---

[78] Cat. of English Bishops, *p.* 217.

[79] Vide Wharton's Notes on Rudb. Ang. Sacra, *vol.* i. *p.* 227.   [80] Ib.

flowing tide not to approach his feet, the extravagance and impiety of their flattery, in extolling his power as equal to that of the almighty Lord of the Ocean. Canute died in the year 1036, and was deposited before the high altar in this Church; five years afterwards the body of his cruel and gluttonous son, Hardicanute, was buried near the same spot.

EDWARD, surnamed the Confessor, from his presumed sanctity, was next exalted to the throne by the general voice of the people; and his coronation was conducted with great splendour in this Cathedral[81]. During his reign a remarkable trial of that mode of judgment practised by the Saxons, called the *fiery-Ordeal*, is recorded to have been made on the person of Queen Emma, who, among other calumnies, had been falsely accused of a criminal intercourse with Bishop Alwyn. This story coming, at length, to the knowledge of the Queen, (who had been treated with much rigour by her son, and obliged to retire to the Abbey of Wherwell, near this city), she insisted on undergoing the proof of her guilt or innocence by the fiery ordeal; and Winchester Cathedral was appointed as the place of trial. Here, in presence of the King, and a crowded assembly of all ranks, she is stated to have walked unhurt, though bare-footed, over nine red hot plough-shares; and in memory of her extraordinary deliverance to have given nine manors to this Church: a similar number is said to have been bestowed by Bishop Alwyn; and three others (those of Portland, Weymouth, and Wyke) by Edward himself, whose indignation against his mother, for marrying Canute, is affirmed to have been removed by this event[82]. Alwyn died in the year 1047, and Queen Emma in 1052: they

---

[81] On this occasion Edward granted a Charter to the Cathedral, ordering the donation of half a mark to the Precentor, or Master of the Choir; and a cask of wine, and a hundred cakes of white bread to the Convent, as often as a King of England should wear his crown within the city of Winchester. The privileges of this grant were subsequently extended to the monasteries of Westminster and Worcester.

[82] The whole story of Queen Emma and the plough-shares (which, to give apparent credibility to the tale, are said to have been buried in the west cloister of the Cathedral,) can be regarded only as a romantic fiction. So far, indeed, as it is now possible to trace its origin, it seems to have first appeared in the guise of poetry; and was sung, with the popular ballads relating to Winchester, in

were both interred in the Cathedral, and are recorded as its special friends and benefactors.

The last Bishop of Winchester, prior to the Norman invasion, was STIGAND, who had been chaplain to Edward the Confessor, and was translated hither, on the death of Alwyn, from Elmham, in Norfolk, a see that was subsequently removed to Norwich[83]. Five years afterwards, on the banishment of Robert Gemeticensis for seditious practices, he was raised to the archbishopric of Canterbury, which he continued to hold in conjunction with Winchester, till the year 1070, (at which time he was formally deposed, with many other prelates,) in a great Council or Convocation of the Clergy, held in this city, under Hermenfride, Bishop of Sion, the Pope's Legate. Stigand is reputed to have been a very subtle and covetous man, and withal rich and powerful, but very unlearned. His principal misfortunes arose from his having had the boldness to appear at the head of the Kentish men, when they assembled in arms at Swanscombe, in Kent, to demand from William the Norman a full confirmation of their ancient liberties; and although that chieftain, in acceding to their request, had engaged never to suffer it to become a ground of offence, yet the displeasure which he hence conceived against Stigand was immoveable. For awhile, however, he concealed his dislike under a specious, yet hypocritical, respect; but almost immediately after the Council had deprived the archbishop of his dignities, he committed him to close imprisonment in Winchester Castle; where, says Godwin, he was " very hardly used, being scarcely allowed meat enough to hold life and soul together." This harsh treatment, (which is thought to have been designedly inflicted, to force him to disclose where his treasures were concealed) is said to have affected his mind; and he died with chagrin, or voluntary

---

the Priory Hall, on the translation of Bishop Orleton to this See, in the year 1338. (Vide Warton's History of English Poetry, *vol.* i. *p.* 89.) Higden, who wrote about the middle of the same century, relates it at length in his Poly-Chronicon; but the more ancient historians, as Ailred Rievallensis, Malmsbury, Dunelmensis, Huntingdon, and Hoveden, are entirely silent on the subject: the principal later writers who mention it are, Brompton, Knighton, Rudborne, and Harpsfield.

[83] See History of Norwich Cathedral, *p.* 12, wherein is some account of Stigand.

famine[84], within a few months after his deprivation. "After his death, a little key was found about his necke, the locke whereof being carefully sought out, shewed a note or direction of infinite treasures hid under ground in divers places: all that the king pursed in his owne coffers[85]." He was buried in this Cathedral; to which, according to the Winchester Annalist[86], he gave a "prodigious large" and costly crucifix, with its attendant images (St. John and the Virgin); but Rudborne[87] says, that the said crucifix was given to the Church by the King, who had found it in Stigand's treasury. It was afterwards placed over the screen at the entrance into the choir.

[84] Cat. of Eng. Bishops, *p.* 72. The grand charges against Stigand were, that he had presumed to wear the pall of his predecessor Gemeticensis, in the See of Canterbury, without having been duly inducted by the Pope; and had also kept possession of the Sees both of Winchester and Canterbury at the same time. The latter crime, however, if such it were, had never been objected against the famous Saints Dunstan and Oswald; the former of whom held Worcester and London together, and the latter Worcester and York. The fact is, that the great Council at Winchester was purposely assembled to deprive the English clergy of their preferments, in order that the same might be bestowed on foreigners. William was the first sovereign who completely subjected the independence of the English church to papal authority.

[85] Cat. of Eng. Bish. *p.* 73.

[86] Angl. Sac. *vol.* i. *p.* 294.   [87] Ibid. *p.* 251.

Chap. II.

HISTORICAL NOTICES OF THE MUNICIPAL STATE, SEE, AND BISHOPS OF WIN-
CHESTER, UNDER THE ANGLO-NORMAN DYNASTY :—ORIGIN AND BUILDING
OF THE PRESENT CATHEDRAL :—DATES AND STYLES OF THE DIFFERENT
PARTS OF THAT EDIFICE.

A NEW and important era in ecclesiastical history was formed under the
Anglo-Norman dynasty, and Winchester was chosen, soon after the conquest, as the place for the assembly of prelates, monks, &c. in different
Synods.   These were formed to give some semblance of justice or can-
dour to the arbitrary proceedings of the Norman bishops.   Lanfranc, late
Abbot of Bec in Normandy, was first advanced to the chair of Canterbury,
from which Stigand had been recently expelled ; Walkelyn, a chaplain and
relation to the late Duke of Normandy, was promoted to Winchester, and
other priests from the Continent were advanced to other English sees and
monasteries.   The politic monarch knew the influence of the clergy over
the people, and therefore prudently and cunningly assigned all or most of
the chief offices to his dependants, relatives, and ostensible friends.   Thus
he very soon obtained an uncontrolled right, or power over " the established
clergy, and treated them as his captives : he destroyed many of their
churches, he stript most, if not all of them, of their rich furniture ; he laid
a taxation of men and arms to serve him in his expeditions, upon the lands
of the bishops and prelates, and obliged them to secular services unknown
to their predecessors ; he caused many churches, with their tithes, to be
converted into lay-fees for the maintaining his military officers and men of
arms ; the tithes of other churches, which were mostly served by English
priests, he caused to be appropriated to abbies, which were governed, if not
filled by Normans[1]." These acts may be regarded as productive of a bold and

---

[1] Johnson's " Ecclesiastical Laws," &c. vol. ii.   Preface to Lanfranc's Canons.

daring reformation, or revolution, in the ecclesiastical government; and, according to Dr. Milner, it was the third of the kind that had occurred in England. Walkelyn, on taking possession of his See, at first proposed to expel all the monks, but Lanfranc urged him rather to continue and govern them strictly by St. Benedict's rule; Simeon, a brother of the bishop, was appointed Prior. In the Councils held at Winchester in 1070, 1071, and 1076, the clergy, with Lanfranc at their head, formed a series of Canons[1], or laws, levelled at the Saxons, and framed to justify and protect themselves. Among the alterations now effected, was the new modelling of the laws, language, and customs of the kingdom. Every thing was to be Norman, and even the English or Saxon language was to be abolished: Winchester was the residence of the court, and we may safely infer, was fully occupied by the officers, priests, and followers of the king. A new royal castle was commenced here: the curfew, or eight o'clock-bell, was first rung at Winton, to warn all persons to retire to bed, or to extinguish fire at that hour: and a command is said to have been issued hence to depopulate the entire tract or district which now forms the New-Forest[3]: that in-

[1] The heads of a few of the Canons will serve to characterise the monastic manners of the times, and the spirit of the legislators:—1. Of Bishops and Abbots coming in by Simonical heresy:—2. Of ordaining men promiscuously, from bribery:—3. Of the life and conversation of such men:—4. Bishops to celebrate councils twice a year; and, 5, have free power over the clergy and laity of their dioceses:—6. Laymen to pay tithes as it is written:—7. That none invade the goods of the church:—8. That clerks and monks be duly reverenced, or offenders to be anathematised:—9. No Bishop to hold two Sees:—10. Corpses not to be buried in churches:—11. Bishops only to give penance for gross crimes. The penances required from *soldiers* are absurd, cruel, and impolitic; and are irreconcileable to the military character of the monarch, who had obtained his post and power by arms. The soldier who killed a man in battle, to do penance for one year; and a year more for every person he knew he had killed.

[3] The extent of the royal command, as to the formation of the forest and sweeping away 22—36—52, or even 60 parish churches, as variously represented, is a subject of dispute with different writers. The old chroniclers assert it, and also represent that the death of the Conqueror's sons, Richard, and William Rufus, and his grandson, Henry, in the New Forest, were all marks of the offended Deity's vengeance for such an impious offence. Some modern authors disbelieve the relation, and show it to be founded in the misrepresentation and exaggeration of those cloistered annalists who hated the monarch, and sought every opportunity to traduce his character. See this subject

quisitorial edict of ascertaining and registering the whole landed property of the realm in the ' *Domesday Book*,' or ' *Roll of Winchester*,' was issued from this city A. D. 1083, and here that important record was kept: but another more material event, as relating to our present subject, and the stability of the See, was the commencement of a large and magnificent *Cathedral*, by the Norman bishop, in 1079. The old historians clearly intimate, that he began the church from its *foundation*, and raised it at his own expence, although the same writers admit, that the former edifice, by Ethelwold, had not been erected more than a century. Some of these also relate that the bishop employed a little finesse at the very beginning of his work, but which, according to Dr. Milner, "proved the greatness of the undertaking, and generosity of the Conqueror." The prelate, wanting timber for his new fabric, solicited some from the monarch, who granted him as much from his wood of Hanepinges, or Hampege, near Winchester, as he could cut down and carry away in *three days*. Taking advantage of this unqualifying grant, he employed all the men, horses, carts, &c. he could obtain, and levelled and carried away the whole of the said wood, or "forest," within the prescribed time. This act, Dr. Milner says, so " prodigiously incensed" the monarch, that he refused to see the bishop; but the latter, in disguise, contrived to obtain an interview, and explained that he had not exceeded the monarch's prescribed *time of three days*, &c. when the king mildly remarked, ' *Most assuredly, Walkelyn, I was too liberal in my grant, and you too exacting in the use made of it*[4].' It appears that this event occurred in the last year of the Conqueror's life; and it is said that the bishop continued the building for seven years after that event, when, 1093, the Church and conventual offices were so near completion, that "almost all the bishops and abbots of England assembled in this city to honour the solemn dedication of them, which took place July 15, being the festival of

fully investigated and developed in " *Beauties of England*," *vol.* vi. *Hampshire*. Gilpin's " Remarks on Forest Scenery,"— and Lewis's " Historical Inquiries concerning Forests and Forest Laws," 4to. 1811.

[4] Annales. Wint. an. 1086.

St. Swithun, the patron saint of the place⁵." The Annalist strangely and mysteriously asserts that on the very next day, the workmen *began* to demolish the ancient fabric, which was completely cleared away within a year, excepting the great altar and one " portico." Thus it is plainly implied, that Ethelwold's church was on a different site to that of Walkelyn's; and if the language of Rudborne is to be understood and believed, the whole edifice was *new built* from the foundation. Walkelyn did not long survive the finishing of his church, but according to the monkish annalist, fell a sacrifice to his devotion to that beloved pile. The second Norman monarch, William Rufus, sent a peremptory order from Normandy, in 1098, to the bishop, requiring an immediate remittance of " *C.C. libras*," an " enormous sum," says Milner, " according to the value of money in those days." This sum could not be readily raised, without sacrificing the treasures of the church, or withholding the accustomed support of the poor. In this predicament the prelate prayed to be released from the miseries of such a life, and accordingly he died within ten days after the summons had been delivered. Rufus therefore seized the revenues of this See as he had previously those of others⁶; but this sacrilegious invasion of ecclesiastical property, according to the same writer, was visited by " divine wrath," and punished by an untimely death. He was killed by an arrow from the bow of one of his associates in the chase, and his body was conveyed in a cart to our Cathedral, " the blood dripping from it all the way," says Malmsbury. It was interred under the tower, " attended by many of the nobility, though lamented by few:" which tower, according to the same author, fell the next year, i. e. 1101; but Annals of Wilton say 1107. " Though I forbear to mention the different opinions on this subject, least I should seem to assent too readily to *unsupported trifles;* more especially as the building might have fallen, through imperfect construction, even though he had never been buried there⁷." Considering the time this was written, and the education

---

⁵ Milner, " History, &c. of Winchester," *vol.* i. *p.* 105, from Ann. Win. an. 1093.

⁶ At the day of his death, says Malmsbury, he held three bishoprics and twelve vacant abbies.

⁷ Malmsbury, " History of the Kings of England," by Sharpe, 4to. 1815.

G

and situation of the writer, this may be regarded as extraordinary language, and expressive of extraordinary sentiments. Had Rudborne been influenced by similar feelings, we should have pursued our narrative with more satisfaction and probability. Immediately on the decease of Rufus, Henry, his younger brother, seized the treasury of the palace, &c. and was readily elected to the vacant throne. Soon afterwards he married Matilda, a descendant of the West Saxon Kings, and promoted WILLIAM GIFFARD, his Chancellor, to this See; but he was not consecrated, nor did he even receive episcopal jurisdiction, till seven years afterwards. This delay arose from the disputes, then existing, " concerning the receiving ecclesiastical *investitures* from lay-persons, by the pastoral staff and ring[8]." Henry I. and Anselm, Archbishop of Canterbury, had long contested this point : but the dispute was settled by a synod in London, which declared that no king, nor lay-hand, should be qualified to invest any bishop or abbot with a pastoral staff or a ring : and Anselm consents " that none elected to any prelacy shall be denyed consecration upon account of the homage which he does to the king[9]." Thus adjusted, our bishop, who had been banished, was recalled and formally instituted and consecrated in 1107. Though he does not appear to have done much for his own church or society, he is complimented for founding the college and church of St. Mary Overy, Southwark, London; a convent of Cistercian[10] monks at Waverley, near Farnham, Surrey ; and also another for Nuns, at Taunton. In 1110 he removed the monks, &c. of the New Minster from the north side of the Cathedral, to a place called Hyde-Meadow, at the northern extremity of the city.

It may not be amiss to notice the state of Winchester about this time. As the residence of the monarch, it was also chosen by many of his chief dependant nobles : here was also the royal treasury, royal mint, repository of public records, episcopal palace and cathedral ; three royal monasteries,

[8] Miln. Win. i. 203.

[9] See Malmsbury's History, &c. and Sharpe's translation, for copies of the supplicatory, persuasive, and argumentative letters written by Pope Pascal to the king and to Anselm, on this subject.

[10] This Order is particularly and very liberally commended by William of Malmsbury. See De Regis, *lib.* v. and Sharpe's translation.

besides other inferior religious houses; and, according to Dr. Milner, "an incredible number of parish churches and chapels." The same author, from Trussel, goes on to represent the extent of the city as "incredible" as its number of churches, by saying that its buildings extended "a mile in every direction further than they do at present; on the north to Worthy; on the west to Week; on the south to St. Cross; and on the east to St. Magdalen's Hill." Although this representation appears a little hyperbolical, yet we can readily believe that Winchester, at its zenith of prosperity, was more populous than at present: in those insecure and warring times, few persons however would raise permanent buildings beyond the protection of the fortified walls and bastion towers[11]. It was about this time that our bishop built his castle at Wolvesey, at the south-east angle of this city, also other castles at his manors of Farnham, Taunton, Merden, Waltham, and Downton.

The civil wars between Stephen and Matilda occasioned new commotions in, and destruction to, Winchester. The usurping monarch, on the death of his uncle, hastened from Boulogne to this city, where his brother, HENRY DE BLOIS, was bishop and Pope's legate; and through the influence of that prelate he seized the treasures of the royal palace, amounting, according to Malmsbury, to 100,000l. in money, besides plate, jewels, &c. He soon afterwards seized the castles of the bishops[12], and committed other violences

[11] The Roman boundary walls of this city must have been strong and lofty at that time. In the year 1125, several persons were summoned from different parts of the realm to assemble at Winchester, to answer certain charges for debasing the current coin; and all were convicted, and sentenced to lose their right hands. Three mint-masters of this city were however found innocent, and acquitted. A standard yard measure was settled by the king at this time, and deposited, with other standards of weight and measure, in this city. Among these was the famed Winchester-bushel. See Whitaker's "History of St. Germans."

[12] In spite of a solemn oath before a council of the nobility at Oxford, swearing "he would not retain vacant prelacies, but fill them with persons canonically elected; that he would not disturb either clergy or laity in the enjoyment of their woods, as the late King Henry had dome; nor sue any body for hunting or taking venison; that he would remit the tax of *Danegeld*," &c. These and many other indulgencies and immunities were promised to the people, and ratified by solemn obligatinos: but the political oaths of this ruler, like those of many others, seem only to have been made for expediency and state policy.

against the clergy, which occasioned the latter to assemble a synod in this
city, August 30, 1139, and remonstrate against such oppressive proceedings.   Our present bishop employed his influence to preserve allegiance to
the monarch, but the latter, disregarding the clergy and citizens, hastened
from them to London, which confirmed the indignation of both classes against
him.   The castle of Winchester was soon seized for the Empress, and after
some struggle with the bishop and his party, the Empress herself was
admitted into the city.   This was only a prelude to civil hostilities; for the
bishop, though at first apparently friendly to the new female monarch, soon
thought it proper to strengthen and fortify his castle of Wolvesey.
This was invested by the Empress's troops, under the command of her
natural brother, the Earl of Gloucester, and her uncle, David, King of
Scotland.   Stephen's military partizans were immediately rallied to
relieve the bishop, and a long protracted scene of warfare ensued.   The
whole city, and all its approaches, were occupied by soldiers.   To repel
his assailants, and punish the citizens, the bishop " caused wild-fire and
combustible matter to be thrown out of his fortified palace, upon the
houses of the townsmen, and reduced a great part of them to ashes.   In
this fire were burnt above twenty churches, besides the nunnery within the
walls, and the abbey of Hyde, without; the bishop laying hold of the
opportunity to seize, for his own use, a golden cross, given to the last of
these convents, by King Canute, set with precious stones, (of which he
made 30 marks of gold and 500 of silver), and three royal diadems, with as
many stands of the purest Arabian gold, adorned with jewels and wrought
in the most curious manner[13]."   In this state of civil discord and slaughter
Winchester continued for seven weeks, during which time the Empress and
her adherents were shut up within the walls of the castle.   On the evening of

[13] Carte's History of England, *vol.* i. *p.* 546, from *Flor. Wig. Cont.*   Stow quotes an authority
which states that forty churches were burnt.   Milner thus enumerates the ravages committed at
this time, " they destroyed, first the adjoining Abbey of St. Mary, then the whole north, which
was infinitely the most populous part of the city ; together with twenty churches, the royal palace,
which had been lately built in that quarter, the suburb of Hyde, with the magnificent monastery of
St. Grimbald, erected there in the preceding reign."

Holy-rood day, the bishop devised a plan to deceive and conquer his opponents. He issued a proclamation that peace should prevail on that sacred festival, and that the gates of the city should be opened. The Empress, with some of her friends, and an escort of forces, escaped early in the morning, but not without a conflict, and some of her best officers were taken prisoners. Dr. Milner, on the authority of " Brompton, Knighton, Trussel, and others," says that the Empress devised the following stratagem to effect her escape from Winchester. After representing herself as dangerously ill for some days, it was proclaimed that she was dead: and that her corpse was to be conveyed, on a horse litter, through the army of the besiegers for interment. She thus escaped the outposts, and then mounting her horse, proceeded with her small retinue to Ludgershall, Devizes, and thence on to Gloucester. The intrigues and duplicity of the bishop at length met with a check by an order from the Pope to relinquish his legatine power, with all its authority and influence. This was a severe blow to his ambition, as he had frequently contested the authority even of the Archbishop of Canterbury. Indeed at one time he petitioned Pope Lucius II. to raise the See of Winchester into an archbishopric[14], and to subject the six Sees of Salisbury, Exeter, Wells, Chichester, Hereford, and Worcester to it, and to make a seventh See of Hyde-Abbey.

From the devastations and disasters which Winchester experienced during these royal and clerical wars, it never recovered ; and from this period it loses the principal part of that interest which arises from exciting the hopes and fears of the reader. In the reign of Henry the Second, it appears that the bishop had fled with his treasures to the Continent, which provoked the monarch to seize on and dismantle his three castles of Wolvesey, Waltham, and Merden[15]: the ruins of Winchester were, however, partly restored, a mayor was appointed to govern its internal police, and

[14] Carte. Hist. Engl. from Mat. Paris and Rudborne. This prelate is said to have been the first to have introduced the practice of appealing to Rome ; " and, on this account, as well as others, deserved very ill of this church and nation." Johnson, *Eccles. Laws.*

[15] Dr. Milner, i. 219, observes, " this can only be understood of the ditches, barbacan, and other outworks.—Rad. Diceto, in his Ymagines, Hist. says the king destroyed all the bishop's six castles."

this was the first town in England thus governed: in the next reign it was invested with the privilege of a corporation, by which it formed " an independent state in the heart of the kingdom." The Abbot of Hyde-Abbey instituted a suit against the bishop to make him account for the grand crucifix, and other valuables, which he had pilfered from that house. The royal treasury was still kept at Winchester, and to that city Richard Cœur-de-Lion hastened after the death of his father, and took possession of valuables to the amount of 900,000l. In this Cathedral he was also solemnly crowned, a second time, on the 17th of April, 1194. This second coronation he demanded, on returning to his kingdom after having suffered imprisonment in the dungeon of Trivallis[16]. On first coming to this city he dispossessed the Cathedral " of its two manors, and the bishop of the royal castle and county of Winchester[17]." The reign of John is distinguished in the Annals of Winchester for some important grants to the city, and by its immediate participation in a violent quarrel, which lasted six years, between the King and the Pope, about the election of STEPHEN LANGTON. This person was forced on the clergy and nation by the Roman Pontiff, who through the medium of Pandulph, the legate, also compelled the king to submit to a mortifying and degraded humiliation to the papal throne. He was next excommunicated; assumed contrition, but only to act with treachery and tyranny; which caused the barons, at the instigation of the Winchester prelate, to confederate against him, and compel him to sign Magna Charta. Winchester was afterwards conquered and occupied by French troops, who committed great devastation on the castles of the king and bishop. Under the next reign and next prelacy, our city was again restored; but towards the end of the reign, much opposition arose between the monarch and monks about the election of a bishop.

Having now furnished a general view of the progressive history of Winchester and its See, up to the beginning of the thirteenth century, we shall direct our whole attention to the Cathedral, its offices and officers. By what has been already stated, it appears that the present church was built

[16] Milner, " from an ancient historian of great credit," gives a particular account of this coronation. Hist. Winchester, i. 240.   [17] Milner, from Rog. Hovedon.

by Walkelyn, " from the foundation ;" but many antiquaries contest this point, and assign parts of it to a *much earlier date.* On this subject I am willing to attend to the opinions and reasonings of all ; and therefore willingly give publicity to the following letter, from the gentleman appointed by the Dean and Chapter to superintend the architectural repairs, &c. of the Church.

" DEAR SIR,
    " I have at length undertaken to arrange, upon paper, the ideas that have from time to time arisen in my mind, relative to the styles and dates of the several parts of that interesting and venerable fabric, the Cathedral Church of this city.

" It is not without much diffidence, that I undertake to express my opinion upon a subject, which has engaged the attention of antiquaries of eminent learning and ingenuity.   I shall, however, find some apology in the consideration that different conclusions have been drawn from the historical information they have collected ; a circumstance which shows that such information, though very essential to our inquiry, cannot be entirely depended upon, without a patient and scrupulous survey of the existing parts of the fabric, which, I believe, it may with confidence be said, will afford ample evidence to warrant us in premising generally, that the ancient historians of the Cathedral, either from misconception of the authorities from which their information was derived, or from their zeal to extol the munificence of the several benefactors to the fabric, must have greatly exaggerated the description of the works performed at different periods.

" Having thus prepared a foundation we shall be able to trace without great difficulty, the works of the illustrious sovereigns and prelates who have been most eminently distinguished by their zeal and munificence, as founders or improvers of this ancient structure, from the commencement of the fourth century down to the period of the Reformation.

" One of the latest historians of this edifice, Dr. Milner, and the authorities he cites, inform us that a basilic of vast extent and magnificence

was erected for the purpose of Christian worship so early as the second
century, upon the site which the Cathedral now occupies: of such an
edifice it cannot be pretended that any part can now remain to be identified, for we are told by the same authority, that after it " had subsisted
about 120 years it was levelled with the ground." It is, however, probable,
as will hereafter be shown, that some part of the foundation of such a
structure may be still existing.

" After the destruction of the first edifice, it is said to have been rebuilt,
from the foundation, no less than four times in the short space of 780
years. The improbability of this seems to have staggered the belief of Dr.
Milner, who relates it; for he tells us it is probable that Ethelwold " not only
made use of the loose materials of the ancient building, but also incorpo-
rated such parts of it as he found of sufficient strength to be left standing;" and the same author, when he speaks of the rebuilding of this vast
structure by Walkelyn, says, " It was not then from any real necessity of
such a work, that our first Norman bishop rebuilt the Cathedral; but the
fact is, the Normans in general, being a high spirited people, held the
Saxons, with all their arts, learning, and whatever belonged to them, in
the most sovereign contempt."

From the historical notices we meet with, we shall find no difficulty in
admitting, that great improvements were made in the fabric of the
Cathedral at, or about, the following stated periods: viz. in the year 313,
" by the contributions of private Christians," when Constans was bishop of
the See; about the year 584, by the Saxon King, Kenewalch; about the
year 980, by Bishop Ethelwold; and again, in the year 1079, by Bishop
Walkelyn, of whom it is particularly recorded, that he built the tower,
which was at that time considered a stupendous work; and that he cut
down the whole of an extensive wood to supply the timber necessary for
the completion of the edifice. This we may readily admit; but when we
attentively compare the architecture, and the workmanship of the tower,
with that of the greater part of the adjoining transept, we shall not hesitate
to ascribe to the latter a much earlier date; for it is not difficult to trace

distinctly, the junction of the Norman with the Saxon work, not only by the superiority of the masonry[18], but by the shape of the arches. The two arches of every story, on each side of the transept next to the tower, and the respective piers between them, were evidently rebuilt with the tower; and this may be considered the extent of Walkelyn's work in masonry, as far as respects the Cathedral. In addition to this, which was certainly a work of considerable magnitude, it may with great reason be admitted, that he entirely new roofed the whole of the transept and nave in a manner that might well entitle it to be termed, new and magnificent; and when we view the greater part of the roof that now remains, we shall not be surprised at what is related of a whole wood being cleared to furnish the timber necessary for the purpose.

" The Norman roof now remaining, is that of the whole of the transept south of the tower, and that of the whole nave west of the tower, with the exception of about fifty feet in length from the west end, which was evidently destroyed by fire; though it is not known at what period, or by what accident the conflagration was occasioned : there is, however, reason to suppose, from the appearance of the timber, as well as from the mode of construction, that this new part of the roof cannot be of higher antiquity than the seventeenth century.

" The roof of the transept, northward of the tower, being of a construction very different from that of the nave, and southern part of the transept, we must conclude that the decay of the Norman roof in that situation was more rapid, and that it required renewal before the other parts; for we cannot suppose that Walkelyn would have left this part incomplete.

" It is presumed that what has been said of the architecture and work-manship of the tower and transept, will prove that some portions of the latter existed previous to the time when Walkelyn is said to have rebuilt it from the ground. It now remains to show, that in the ancient parts there now exists the clearest evidence of additions to the fabric, at a period still

---

[18] The improved workmanship of the Norman builders may be most clearly seen in the facing of the stone, and also in the joints, where the mortar is not equal to a fourth part of that used in the Saxon work.

H

more remote; this is to be seen in the design, rather than in the execution of the work. The alteration now speaking of, was probably the work of Ethelwold, and consisted of an increase of the substance, and alteration of the shape, of four principal pillars of the transept, unquestionably for the purpose of supporting a tower at the extremity of each of the side ailes. It may be objected, that there is no historical notice or tradition of the existence of such towers, but the evidence of the present state of the structure is of the most decisive nature; for the imposts of the arches which supported the flanks of such towers, are now to be seen distinctly in the spaces between the roof and vaulting of the ailes; and whoever examines with due attention the side arches of the third story of the transept, will perceive that those nearest the extremities, (into which windows have been introduced) were not originally windows, but open arches of communication within the edifice, similar to those between the body and ailes.

" We now come to the investigation of the work of a period still more remote, which is the *Crypt*, under the part of the church between the high altar and the Virgin Chapel. The workmanship in this crypt, though plain and simple in its design, is far superior to any that is to be seen in the whole edifice, excepting those parts which will be hereafter spoken of as the works of de Lucy and Fox. This work is as much superior to that of the greater crypt, to which it adjoins, as the Norman is to the Saxon work in the transept; but its inferior dimensions seem to indicate that it is not the work of the high-spirited Walkelyn, and the circular termination shows it is not the work of a much later period; we may therefore conclude that this is a remnant of the work of our pious British or Roman ancestors, in the early part of the fourth century: and in conformity with the observations before made upon the existing appearances of the fabric, as well as with the historical notices mentioned by Milner, and his authorities, we may proceed to define the works of the various builders from that period down to the eleventh century in the following portions.

" The work of King Kenewalch, now remaining, may be supposed to include the first story of the transept, with the exception of the part before described as being rebuilt by the Norman bishop, and some other innovations in the windows: we may also conclude, that much of the work of that sovereign remains in the pillars of the nave, though they have since been re-moulded, and probably much repaired, in prosecuting the works of the munificent prelate, Wykeham.

"It may be observed, that in the transept a new set off appears at the base of the second tier of Saxon arches, to which it is presumed the work of Kenewalch was taken down by Bishop Ethelwold, and that the work of the latter was continued from thence upwards, to the height of the present parapet, including the towers before spoken of, as well as an increase in the length of the nave; the whole length of which is evidently of Saxon workmanship, as appears by the columns that continue above the vaulting, where the masonry is of the same coarse kind as that before described, in contradistinction to the Norman work. The further work of Ethelwold may be seen in the greater Crypt, upon which he of course added a superstructure, though the work now standing over that foundation is of a much later date, which will be spoken of in its place. With respect to timber roofing, we must suppose that Ethelwold made use of such as he found upon the old building, for when we admit so great a part to have been renewed by Walkelyn, we cannot suppose that he rejected what had been new within the short space of one hundred years, when we find that which he used has endured more than seven hundred years. Milner tells us positively, that Ethelwold first enriched the Cathedral 'with its subterraneous crypts which it before had wanted :' this is certainly at variance with what I have suggested relative to the lesser Crypt; to reconcile which it may be presumed that Milner's authority (which in that instance is not cited) may have meant that the Cathedral was deficient in that respect, or that it wanted crypts proportionate to the general scale of the edifice, and not that it had no crypt. We now come to the work of Walkelyn, which, it is presumed, has been sufficiently proved to be confined to the building of the central Tower and such parts of the edifice as immediately abutted upon it, and to the new roofing of the transept and nave.

"I agree with Dr. Milner in the supposition that Walkelyn's work did not extend eastward of the present tower, but a considerable part of the Saxon edifice remained standing in that situation, including the smaller Tower which Rudborne informs us fell upon Rufus's tomb. The tower thus mentioned I conceive to have been one of those which stood at the eastern extremity of each of the side ailes of the choir, similar to those I have before described as once terminating the side ailes of the transept. An examination of the crypt will show that additions had been made to the walls of the substructure, at a period subsequent to their first erection, which cannot easily be accounted for, otherwise than for the support of the towers thus assigned to that situation; and the fall of one of them towards Rufus's tomb may be reasonably accounted for from the evident circumstance of the foundation in that direction being less substantial than that of the opposite side.

" Before we come to an examination of the works of Bishop de Lucy, it may be observed, that an architectural innovation, probably one of the first specimens of the *pointed arch* in this country, as an integral ornament, is to be seen in the wall inclosing a part of the south-west aile of the transept. This work may be reasonably attributed to Bishop *de Blois:* it seems to appear as an experiment to try the effect of the pointed arch, compared with the semicircular one, and it is curious to observe the predilection that seems to have prevailed in favour of the former, as that is placed in a situation to be viewed with greater advantage than the other, and is also more prominently ornamented.

" We now come to *the work of de Lucy*, in the consideration of which we are again interrupted by a tower of the old Saxon Church, that was left standing in the part eastward of the choir by Walkelyn; and this occasions some difficulty in understanding what was the state of that part of the fabric when de Lucy began his work; for we are to recollect, that the weather-cock falling from the tower in the year 1214, broke the shrine of St. Swithun, which, Dr. Milner justly observes, must have stood near the high altar, and was not likely to have been struck by a heavy body falling from the present tower. We may therefore attribute this accident to the failure of one of the old towers, before described as having stood at

the extremities of the side ailes of the choir, in which situation the high
altar must have been placed nearly between them. The difficulty which
next occurs is to find the situation of the *tower* so particularly stated to
have been begun and finished in the year 1200. The works of this munificent prelate, now remaining, will, I conceive, justify a conclusion that a
tower built under his direction would have been of sufficient strength to have
continued to the present time; nor have we any reason to believe him so
deficient in judgment as to have placed it in a situation to interfere with
any future improvement of the part containing the high altar, which must
at that time have been the most ancient part of the whole fabric: by these
considerations we shall be induced to look for de Lucy's tower at the
eastern part of his work, and we may therefore accordingly recognize a
portion of it in the western part of the present Lady Chapel, which has
evidently been of greater height at some former period than it is at present;
as part of the staircases that led to another story are now to be traced,
though they are nearly filled up by rough masonry in effecting subsequent
alterations.

" With respect to the other works executed by de Lucy, there is some
reason to suspect, however extraordinary it may appear, that he did not
absolutely take down the whole walls of that part of the Church situated
between the old high altar and his new tower, but that the upper part of the
ancient walls were by some means supported while the arches and pillars
were inserted under them; for there are indications of those walls having
been ornamented, above the present vaulting, with sculpture of a very singular pattern, which is so situated that it can hardly be considered as the
accidental application of old materials re-used; it may, however, be
observed, that in all (even the most ancient) parts of the fabric old
materials, exhibiting mutilated mouldings, and other ornaments, are to be
seen indiscriminately used in the successive repairs and alterations, from
the time of the Saxons down to a very late period.

" In returning to the work of de Lucy, we may see cause to believe that
a considerable alteration was made in his plan after his decease, at which
time the work had not probably proceeded further than the vaulting of the

central aile, or nave of that part of the Church, and the walls of the small chapels north and south of the then new tower, or Lady Chapel : the width of these small chapels I conceive to be the width intended by de Lucy for his whole work, as by adhering to this he would have preserved the ancient proportions, which were evidently violated by increasing that width to meet the extreme width of the second Saxon edifice. The ill effect of this innovation is to be seen in various ways ; first, in the disproportionate appearance of the side ailes, compared with the centre, or nave ; secondly, in the defective state of the walls, which are forced much out of their perpendicular by the pressure of the vaulting of the side ailes of such extraordinary width : this failure, however, may be partly attributed to the circumstance of the outer walls being built upon new ground, while the opposite pillars stood upon the solid foundation of the ancient crypt ; and thirdly, in the unequal and unfinished appearance of the east ends of the ailes ; but although these defects occurred in the design, it must be observed, that the workmanship of this period far surpassed any thing that preceded it : the joints in the masonry are hardly to be perceived, and no stroke of a tool is to be seen on the surface ; the mouldings are wrought with accuracy, and the foliage of the capitals is sculptured with boldness and elegance. The *staircases* contained in the two turrets of the eastern ends of these ailes are, I believe, unique : they certainly exceed every thing I have seen or heard of in that way. One hardly knows which to admire most, the elegance of the design or the accuracy of the execution : I imagine those staircases must have led to some offices frequented by superiors of the establishment.

" It does not appear from any historical notice that I have met with, that any considerable repair, or improvement, was made in the Cathedral after the completion of Bishop de Lucy's undertaking till the time of William de Edington ; a prelate who, Dr. Milner says, was ' in his virtues and talents only inferior to Wykeham himself,' and ' that justice has never been done to the memory of this benefactor of our Cathedral.' This passage seems to insinuate that Edington must have executed other works than those described by Bishop Lowth in his Life of Wykeham ; and here it may be observed, that another writer upon ecclesiastical architecture, the Rev. J. Dallaway, in one of the tables at the end of his work, purporting to exhibit the dates, dimensions, and names of the founders of the various parts of the English Cathedrals, mentions the building of the choir of our Cathedral, 138 feet in length and 86 in width; and also the Lady Chapel, 54 feet in length, as the works of Edington in the year 1350.   The same table mentions the tower, 133 feet high, as the work of Godfrey de Lucy, in the year 1190 ; and the presbytery, 93 feet long, and 86 wide, as the work of T. Langton, in the year 1493.   Here we find the dates correspond with other accounts of the times when the respective prelates held the see.   The part of this statement, relative to the work of de Lucy, certainly appears to be at variance with other accounts, which seem to be admitted as authentic, and are corroborated by the style of the architecture; but that part which relates to Edington, though no authority is cited, appears worthy of consideration, as I am not aware of any authentic account relative to that part of the fabric.   For though Dr. Milner, speaking of the part of the Cathedral ' between the tower and the low ailes of de Lucy,' says, ' that great and good prelate, Fox, undertook to rebuild it ;' yet I cannot suppose that a person so well acquainted with the various styles of ancient architecture could mean, that the pillars and arches of the presbytery, with the windows over them, could have been executed by the same persons, or in the same age, as those of the side ailes adjoining; those works are in reality very different, both in design and in execution, and I am therefore inclined to believe that Mr. Dallaway has obtained some information upon the point that escaped the industrious researches of Dr. Milner.   From these circumstances, and from the appearance of the work itself, it seems highly probable that the part between the tower and the altar-screen was built by Edington, and that the Stalls in the choir were also the work of the same prelate, or of his executors; for upon minute inspection it may be found that there are many similarities in the execution of these works, and those about his tomb and its inclosure.   I pass by, at present, the part between the altar screen and the work of de Lucy, considering that to be

the work of another benefactor, and proceed to the west end of the fabric,
where I agree with Dr. Milner, that Edington, or his executors, completed
' the two first windows from the great west window, with the corresponding buttresses, and one pinnacle on the north side of the church; as likewise the first window towards the west, with the buttress and pinnacle on
the south side.' I am further of opinion, that the two west windows of the
side ailes were executed at the same time, and probably the two hexagonal
turrets; these certainly appear to have been carried as high as the present
parapet before any alteration was made in the design in consequence of
Wykeham's undertaking, as it may be seen that a cornice, evidently
intended to have been continued from the turrets along the outer wall of the
nave, is suddenly broken off, and another cornice begun, at some height
above it. It is also evident that the sloping parapets, running from the
hexagonal turrets, over the windows of the west end of the ailes, are carried
several feet higher than they were designed to be by Edington; as part of
the course of stone, intended to project over the junction of the lead
covering of the roof, with the inside of the wall, is now to be seen; by
which we discover that the small moulding upon the second ornamented
space over the window was intended as the extreme height of that part.
The nature of the ornaments in the parts now under consideration was
certainly calculated to justify the observations of Bishop Lowth, that ' in
the year 1371 some work of this kind was carrying on at a great expense;'
but whether it included the great western window or not, is doubtful. I
am of opinion that the sum provided by Bishop Edington was expended
before the intended work was completed, for whatever was done at that
time must have fallen far short of what was really necessary; since we are
informed by Bishop Lowth, that upon Wykeham's visitation of the Cathedral in 1393[19], ' the fabric of the Church was greatly out of repair, and
the estates allotted to that use were very insufficient for it. The bishop
ordered, that the Prior for the time being, should pay 100*l.* a year for seven
years ensuing, and the Sub-prior and Convent 100 marks in like manner, for

[19] Lowth's Life of Wykeham, third edit. *p.* 193.

this service; over and above the profits of all estates so allotted, and all gifts and legacies.' Now it is difficult to conceive, that the nave or ailes could, at that time, have been so much dilapidated as to call for this extra-ordinary injunction, when we see the transept at this time so nearly in its original state; we must therefore attribute the defect to the unfinished state of the work begun by Edington.

" We now come to an investigation of the improvements made in this venerable structure by a prelate justly celebrated for the profound skill and taste displayed in the various works executed under his auspices, and through his boundless munificence. In the subject before us we view the last *work of William of Wykeham*, commenced in the 70th year of his age, and prosecuted with diligence throughout the remaining ten years of his life; though it is to be regretted that we cannot with certainty deter-mine the extent of the work executed during that time. Dr. Milner has discovered that Wykeham did not absolutely take down so much of the ancient fabric as his learned biographer supposed he did, and this we may readily admit; but it is to be observed, that Bishop Lowth quotes Rud-borne as his authority, and if Dr. Milner has himself been mistaken respecting what he represents as the work of Bishop Fox, we shall not feel much difficulty in supposing that similar mistakes have arisen respecting the extent of the works executed at more distant periods by Ethelwold and Walkelyn, as previously assumed. In proceeding to trace the works of Wykeham, we have an unerring guide in the Bishop's own Will, as far as it is applicable to this purpose. By it we find, that within fifteen months previous to his decease, so much of his undertaking remained unfinished that he directed 3000 marks to be applyed for its completion (a sum far exceeding what he had formerly directed the prior and convent to expend in seven years): and we find by his directing the walls, the windows, and the vault to be finished throughout according to the new mode in which he had already completed some parts on the south side, that a considerable part on the north side still remained unfinished: but as we find no mention of the great west window, we may conclude that he commenced his work in that part. I have before expressed some doubt whether this window

I

was the work of Edington, or Wykeham ; but when it is considered **that** there is a peculiarity in the upper compartment very unlike any part of Edington's, and invariably followed through the whole of Wykeham's windows ; and when we see the outer face of the wall over the window, and the face of the wall making the gable end of the roof, ornamented with mouldings and compartments accordant with the known taste of Wykeham, we can hardly hesitate to pronounce it his work : we may also with confidence attribute to him the judicious and elegant alteration of the Saxon pillars, the whole of the windows of the nave and of the ailes, (excepting those before attributed to Edington,) and the vaulting of the ailes with which the flying buttresses are so ingeniously combined for resisting the pressure of the greater vault.   But when we compare the vaulting of the ailes with that of the nave, stupendous as we must acknowledge the latter to be, we cannot but feel that the former presents a much more finished appearance, and that the genius of Wykeham had ceased to direct the operation.   The vault of the nave may therefore be considered as the work of Wykeham's executors, probably assisted by his successor, *Cardinal Beaufort,* who is described by Dr. Milner as a great benefactor to the Cathedral, though he does not particularize his works.   I think it highly probable, that in addition to a share in the vaulting of the nave, the Cardinal erected the *Portals* which make so fine a feature in the western façade ; and that he also added the two side windows, eastward of the altar screen, as well as the Screen itself, and the beautiful row of canopies facing eastward, in Bishop de Lucy's part of the Church, as I conceive those to be works of an earlier date than Bishop Fox, to whom Dr. Milner ascribes them ; besides the works of Fox are always to be known by his arms and devices, of which these inimitable specimens of art are quite destitute.

" When *William of Waynflete* succeeded Beaufort in the See, we may presume that the Cathedral was in the most satisfactory state of repair ; as we do not find by his biographer, Dr. Chandler, that he undertook any repair or embellishment of the fabric, except his own sepulchral Chantry. We may, however, be assured, that a prelate possessing in so eminent a degree the liberality as well as the talents of his great predecessor,

Wykeham, would not have withheld his assistance, if any part of the fabric had remained in an unfinished state. It cannot be necessary for me to say any thing of a monument so well known as the chantry of this prelate, further than to express my opinion that as it would not be desirable to see in that situation an exact copy of its opposite neighbour, the stately and well executed sepulchral chantry of Beaufort, so it would be extremely difficult, if not impossible, to devise a more elegant and fit companion for it.

"The next work in chronological order is the alteration and addition to the *Lady Chapel*, which Dr. Milner sufficiently proves to have been executed by the *Priors, Hunton* and *Silkstede*, though the latter may probably have been assisted by Bishop Courteney. The old part of the Lady Chapel must have been previously vaulted, as appears by the disposition of the ornaments on the east and west sides: we cannot say much in praise of this work of good Prior Silkstede, as far as respects the vaulting, the columns, and the windows, though the ornaments below the windows, both outside and within, are entitled not only to notice but to admiration, as well for the design as for the execution; and of the linings and fittings of this chapel, in carved oak, it is impossible to speak in terms that can do justice to the subject. The chastness of the design will, I believe, be generally considered to have a more pleasing effect than the profusion of ornaments spread over the neighbouring Chapel, which was fitted up by Bishop Langton about the same time, for his sepulchral chantry, and exhibits many beautiful specimens of carved oak, though they are rather too much crowded to be seen with advantage. This chapel, however, as well as the opposite one on the north side, appears to have been previously occupied as private oratories; as there are ranges of niches in the eastern walls, of a style at least as early as the time of Bishop Edington.

"It now remains to point out the works of *Bishop Fox*, the last who has been distinguished by any extensive repair or improvement of the fabric of the Cathedral; and though we may not ascribe to this prelate the whole of the works supposed by some to have been executed by him, yet it must be acknowledged, that in taste, in skill, and in munificence, he is entitled to be considered as the worthy successor of Wykeham and of Waynflete. His works in the Cathedral I conceive to be the two turrets at the eastern extremity of the presbytery, with the magnificent window between them, and the whole of the ornamented wall over it, terminating with an elegant tabernacle ornamented by the pelican, his favourite emblem, and containing his statue, in stone. It ought not to escape observation, that the outside label of this window springs from two corbel busts, representing a king and a bishop, both finely sculptured, and in the highest state of preservation: and when it is considered that the art of sculpture was at that time in a flourishing state, it is probable that these busts may be true portraits of King Henry the Seventh and of Bishop Fox. The timber-framed Vaulting of the presbytery is also the undoubted work of Fox, and in this, as well as in the east window, he has shown great taste and judgment, by consulting the models before him, in the western window and in the vaulting of the nave, upon both of which he has improved. It is also unquestionable that this prelate rebuilt, from the foundation, (that is from the walls of the crypt,) the whole of the Ailes, north and south of the presbytery, including their windows, roofing, and stone vaulting, with the flying buttresses and pinnacles, the whole of which was executed in the most perfect style of workmanship. The open Screens between the presbytery and ailes may be considered as the completion of this prelate's work, excepting his own Chantry, which is certainly a master piece of its kind, equally calculated to display an elegance of taste in design, and the perfection of art in its execution. The successive prelates from Edington to Langton (with the exception of Courteney, who presided but a short time in this lucrative See,) had erected or adorned sumptuous chantries in the varied styles of the times in which they respectively flourished, and Fox seems to have determined not to make a chasm in the series of works that are at once calculated to delight the admirers and instruct the practitioners in art. This accomplished prelate, as was before observed, had succeeded in improving upon models presented to his contemplation in his own Cathedral, but in this instance he seems to have despaired of doing so, and therefore to have studied the work of his contemporary, Bishop

Audley, in the Cathedral of Salisbury; and in this it will, I believe, be admitted, that he has also improved upon his model: and this is the last work executed in our Cathedral in the fascinating style called Gothic.

" The opposite Chapel, erected by *Bishop Gardiner*, has only the merit of occupying a space nearly similar to that of Fox's, but its architecture clearly discovers that the revolution in religion was accompanied by as sudden a revolution in art. It is really astonishing, in viewing this chapel, to observe, that although some part of it was intended to imitate the work of Fox, yet the execution of that part is incredibly mean.

" There appears to have been an attempt to return to the former style in the time of Charles the First, when the ceiling was made in that part of the choir under the tower, and the canopy placed over the communion table; but those attempts were not more successful than that to complete the tower over the entrance to Christ-Church tower at Oxford.

" Of Inigo Jones's justly celebrated Screen, I can only say, that I should admire it in another situation; and wishing that before you have completed your series of Cathedrals, you may see something more appropriate in its place,   I remain, dear Sir,

Yours, &c.

Winchester, Dec. 29, 1817.   W. GARBETT."

I have given publicity to the preceding ingenious and original remarks by my intelligent correspondent, respecting the ages of different parts of the building, because the whole evidently emanates from a mind intimately acquainted with the subject; and because I am aware that many persons, as well as Mr. Garbett, are of opinion that parts of the present fabric of Winchester Cathedral, are true specimens of Saxon architecture, and raised by the Saxons before the Norman conquest. Some of these persons, however, very unlike my correspondent, are influenced more by wayward fancy than judgment,—are impelled to believe and assert, whatever their prepossessions and prejudices incline them to—and are always endeavouring to reduce the styles and ages of buildings to favourite theories, instead of seeking for ample evidence to authenticate dates. It is also a favourite maxim with some of these gentlemen to carry back the date of every church, as far as possible, as if they thereby derived a peculiar pleasure, or advantage; and like the late Mr. King and Mr. Carter, they do not hesitate to assert, peremptorily, that the oldest part must be of the age of its first foundation. To such persons, who prefer fiction to fact, and romance to history, it is useless to argue, and impertinent to urge the claims of rationality and common sense. Still, however, as the impartial student seeks for faithful information in such a work as the present, and is entitled to expect the candid opinions of the author on a controverted subject, I feel it my duty to explain my own opinion, and the reasons on which that is founded.

Respecting the origin of the present fabric, the statement of Rudborne is as conclusive as language can render it. He asserts—and we must suppose from documents belonging to the church—that Walkelyn began to *rebuild*, or *re-edify* it from the foundation, in 1079[20]: and on the 6th ides of April, anno 1093, he says that the new fabric was completed and re-dedicated. He proceeds to say, that on the day following the feast of St. Swithun, the bishop's men began to break down the old monastery, and which was *demolished within the year*, excepting one porch, or portico, and the great altar[21]. If this evidence be not sufficiently conclusive, we shall derive much collateral proof from comparing the style and character of the arches, columns, capitals, and bases; the windows, buttresses, mouldings, and piers of this Church, with such buildings as are admitted to have been raised by the Normans. Of these many remain so precisely similar to the crypts, transepts, and remaining part of the chapter-house at Winchester, that we must conclude they were erected at the same time, and by contemporary builders. Besides, we are repeatedly told that the Normans were a proud, aspiring, pompous people; eager to make every thing new in their

[20] Anno MLXXIX. Walkelinus Episcopus a fundementis Wintoniensem cœpit recædificare ecclesiam." Ang. Sac. i. 294.

[21] " Sequenti vero die Domini Walkelini Episcopi cœperunt homines primum vetus frangere Monasterium; et fractum est totum in illo anno, excepto portico uno, et magno altari." Ang. Sac. i. 295.

newly acquired territory, and to impress all their works with their own national marks; they were also equally prompt to sweep away all traces of the arts, and customs of the people they subjugated. These considerations, and others which might be adduced, make me conclude that no architectural part of the present church, is strictly Saxon. Some of the foundation walls are probably, and merely probably, anterior to the Norman conquest: but as expense and labour were secondary objects with such men as Walkelyn, and Gundulph of Rochester; and as their edifices were intended to be *much larger* than those of their predecessors, we can scarcely believe that they would make use of even their foundations. It is true there are some variations in the masonry, i. e. in the joints and courses of the stones in the extreme ends, and the more central parts of the transepts; but this might have arisen from different workmen, who were employed even at the same time, and still more from those who were engaged on the Church at different periods of its erection; for it cannot be doubted that an edifice of this size must have been some years in progress, and that many masons were unquestionably employed in its construction.

The dates assigned by Mr. Garbett to the other parts of the Church are mostly in unison with my own opinions; on two or three points we are, however, at issue, and in describing those members of the building, on which we differ, I shall make free to offer a few remarks.

Still, although I cannot satisfy my own mind, or persuade myself that Winchester Church contains any decided specimens of early Anglo-Saxon architecture, I am aware that many other persons may feel perfectly convinced: and may perceive clear proof of remote antiquity in the styles of arches, and in the masonry. On such obscure subjects there will be difference of opinion, and this difference will most probably lead to truth. My mind, I own, is extremely scrupulous, and requires something bordering on palpable demonstration. Knowing that many persons have deceived themselves, and then imposed on the world, by precipitancy and credulity; I have persuaded myself that caution, and rational scepticism, on historical subjects, are necessary to constitute the impartial antiquary.

Chap. III.

DESCRIPTION OF THE FORM, ARRANGEMENT, AND CONSTRUCTION OF THE
CHURCH:—ALSO OF ITS EXTERIOR AND INTERIOR BEAUTIES AND DEFECTS,
WITH REMARKS ON ITS STYLES OF ARCHITECTURE:—AND ON THE VARIOUS
PORTIONS OF THE EDIFICE, WITH REFERENCE TO THE ACCOMPANYING
PLATES.

THE Cathedral Church of Winchester has been called '*a school of ecclesiastical architecture,*' and with some degree of propriety: for as a school
is intended to instruct novices in any branch of art or science, so this edifice
is calculated to display to the student an interesting and varied series of
examples of the ancient architecture of England, from an early age up to
a recent period. Here therefore he may study styles, dates, and those
varieties which peculiarly belong to the sacred buildings of the middle ages.
He will also find, in this edifice, some very interesting examples of construction, in the walls, vaulting, and other parts of the masonry and
carpentry: all of which are as essential to the scientific architect as the
art of designing and planning a building. If we fail to satisfy ourselves
as to Roman remains, or genuine Saxon work—if, after a careful
examination, we retire either doubtful, or persuaded there is no such
architecture, still we shall have ample evidence and examples of Norman
works. The plans and magnificent designs of those proud invaders, and
innovators, are amply set forth in this fabric. We see that they built for
themselves and for posterity; that their edifices were solid and substantial;
simple in their forms, and large in their parts:—that as their religion was
intended to awe, terrify, and soothe the mind, so its primary temple was
calculated most essentially to promote these ends. Vieing with Gundulph,
and other Norman prelates, Walkelyn seems to have designed his Cathedral
on a scale of grandeur to equal, or surpass, all the others in the island;
and although we are not informed by what means he carried his designs

into effect, we are assured that he raised nearly the whole of the Church in his life-time. A large portion of his work is now standing; but much of it has been altered, and more is obscured.

From what has been already related, it appears that not only a Church, but the necessary offices for a prior and monks, were erected by the first norman bishop. Nearly every architectural member of the latter has been swept away, as well as the cloisters, chapter-house, and other appendages[1]. The Church, however, remains for our admiration and enquiry; and at present consists of the following members :—a nave, with two ailes, a transept to the north and another to the south of a central tower, each having ailes at the sides and extreme ends ;—a choir, and a presbytery with side ailes ;—a space, east of the altar, consisting of three ailes, all of nearly equal width and height ;—a lady chapel, east of the latter;—two chantry chapels to the north and south of the lady chapel ;—three distinct crypts beneath the east end of the Church, and five other chantries.

The *Exterior* of Winchester Cathedral presents few beauties, or attractive features. Its length of nave, plainness of masonry, shortness and solidity of tower, width of east end, and boldness of transepts, present so many peculiar and specific characteristics. Although the architectural antiquary seeks in vain for that picturesque arrangement of parts, and successive variety, which belong to the Cathedrals of Salisbury, Lincoln, Wells, &c. yet he soon discovers a peculiar grandeur from its extent and quantity; and also many specific features of design, which tend to rouse and gratify inquiry. As a *distant object* the Church presents a large and long mass of building. Its nave, particularly as seen from the south, is distinguished by its length of roof and extent of unbroken lines; and the low, stunted tower, as Gilpin remarks, " gives the whole building an air of heaviness[2]."

[1] In the Deanery House, and in one of the Prebendal Houses, south of the Church, are some columns, arches, and vaulted roofs to certain rooms on the ground floor.

[2] The same author, who is generally judicious, and often elegantly apposite in his comments, uses some strange and absurd language in speaking of this Church. He says, " I doubt whether a *spire* was ever intended," when there was no reason either to doubt, or to question the subject; as spires were not known when this tower was built. Again, he asks " Why the tower, *in the hands* of so *elegant* an architect, [Wykeham] was left so ill-proportioned, is a question of surprise." Now the tower was never *in the hands*, nor subjected to the improvements, of this clerical architect.

K

The whole Church is seated in a valley, and on three of the approaches to the city is seen from high ground.   On the east and west the hills are much higher than the top of the tower, and consequently the building is viewed to great disadvantage.   The eastern end, however, with its pinnacles, turrets, flying buttresses, and tower, form a fine and pleasing group.   From the Portsmouth and Alton roads, i. e. approaching it from the S. E. and N. E. the Church is seen to rise above the contiguous houses and trees in massive, bold, and picturesque features.

The *Interior*, however, will amply compensate for any defects or deficiencies of the outside.   This presents several architectural and sculptural excellencies: this displays a variety of truly interesting and important subjects, for professional and critical examination.   Whilst the fine and sublime architecture of Wykeham, in the Nave and ailes, produces the most impressive effect, and claims general admiration ; the substantial, plain, and large works of Walkelyn, in the tower and transepts, are imposing and simply grand.   In the north Transept, lately cleaned and restored, we see the effect and character of this style, in nearly its pristine state.   Every member is in unison with the rest: each is large, bold, and unadorned.   The bases, capitals, clustered columns, or piers, and the single shafts, are devoid of all ornament, and appear to be entirely designed for their proper places and necessary uses.   The arches, likewise plain, are composed of squared stones, and formed wholly for strength and utility, without any pretension to beauty.   On the contrary, in the carving of the *Stalls*, and the wood-work of the Lady Chapel and Langton's Chapel, we see a redundancy of ornament prevail.   The designers seem to have wantoned in a licentiousness of fancy, and thought they could not surcharge their works with too much variety, or introduce an excess of decoration.   Still these parts of the edifice afford us much delight, even from this very caprice. The eye wanders from one form and object to another, in search of novelty, and the mind is kept in constant and pleasing exertion by analizing and appropriating the whole.   The elaborate and sumptuous *Altar-Screen* is full of architectural members, and is certainly very beautiful.   It is covered with niches, canopies, buttresses, pinnacles, crockets, pediments, &c. and when in its original colour and condition, with statues and costly ornaments, must have been surprisingly splendid. The monumental *Chantries* for Fox, Beaufort, Waynflete, Wykeham, and Edington, have all their peculiar beauties, and each presents a specific style in design and detail: that of Edington has, perhaps, the least interest as a whole; but its statue is the most elegant of any in the Church. Wykeham's altar-tomb, and some of its interior parts, are fine specimens of the age; Fox's chantry is a superb example of monumental architecture; gorgeous in its design, and exquisite in execution. Those for Beaufort and Waynflete seem placed in opposition to each other, like rival beauties, to court admiration: each consists of a pyramidical series of canopies, crocketed pinnacles, niches, tracery, buttress piers, &c. raised on, and supported by, open arches, piers, and panelled screens. Each also occupies a corresponding arch, and each is formed to enshrine and surmount the altar tombs and statues of the deceased prelates. It may be confidently asserted, that the combined group of chantries, screens, and clustered columns, in this part of Winchester Church, is not equalled by any spot in England, or in Europe. Its full effect, as first discovered to the stranger, is represented in *Plate* XVII. and comprehends the chantries of Fox, a; Beaufort, c; and Waynflete, b; with the Chapels of Langton, e; and the Lady Chapel, d. Every remove of the spectator, as he wanders round this part of the building, presents these objects differently grouped, differently combined, and with varied effects of light and shade. With such a splendid feast before him, it is not to be wondered if the architectural enthusiast, indulges himself to excess, and almost satiates his senses.

The foregoing subjects may be regarded as the pre-eminent beauties of the Church; but still there are many others to claim the attention of different persons, accordingly as they are influenced by particular studies or partialities. Most of these will come under notice in the following description of the principal divisions and parts of the fabric.

The *Nave* and its ailes are distinguished by the uniform style of the whole; in solid and elegant piers, arches, windows, sculptured bosses, &c. "This," says Gilpin, "is perhaps the most magnificent nave in England." The Transepts and Tower next claim attention, as unrivalled specimens of

Norman architecture. Solid masses of masonry, vast spaces in height and width, with very little ornament, are the distinguishing features of those portions of the edifice. The transepts are open to the timber roof, and thus appear very lofty: but the effect of the rafters, and ragged timbers, is offensive. It presents the idea of neglect and ruin, and thus, when contrasted with the solidity and uniform beauty of the nave, makes a very unfavourable impression on the mind. In the southern transept, the aile to the west and south, is entirely excluded by a wall, which fills up the whole of the arches; and the eastern aile is divided into three different chapels, or chantries, by screens, between each, and also between them and the centre of the transept. The northern Transept is less encumbered and less obscured: its centre, east and north ailes, the triforium, and clerestory, are all clear and open to inspection; but the western aile is a place of lumber, and its arches are walled up. [See Plate xii.] The *Choir* and eastern end are elevated above the nave and ailes by an ascent of several steps; and in this portion of the building the stranger will perceive several different styles of architecture, and several different subjects to arrest his attention, and demand his admiration. The choir occupies a space mostly beneath the Norman tower, and is fitted up with a series of elaborately carved stalls on the west, north, and south sides. In the carvings of basso-relievo, finials, crockets, and misereres, there are many grotesque designs, as well as many specimens of very fine workmanship. At the north-eastern extremity of the choir is the *Pulpit*, a very curious piece of carved-work, and evidently executed for Prior *Silkstede*, whose name is twice repeated on it. On the same side of the choir, beneath one of the lofty arches of the tower, is the Organ, which thus occupies an unusual place. Nearly facing the pulpit is the Bishop's Stall, or throne, a very incongruous and absurd piece of workmanship, presented by Bishop Trelawny, and intended as an ornamental appendage: but, like the screen between the nave and choir, it is formed in the Roman or classical style, as commonly termed, and therefore becomes an unsightly object. Between the choir and altar is a large open space, called the *Presbytery*, which is separated from the ailes by stone screens, and from the altar by a carved railing. Immediately behind the altar screen is an open space, formerly a chapel, and inclosed by the splendid chantry of Fox, on the south, that of Gardiner, to the north, the altar-screen on the west, and another screen to the east. All these objects are highly interesting to the architectural antiquary, and will be hereafter described. East of these is a large open space, consisting of three ailes of nearly equal width and height, and inclosing the very elaborate and elegant chantry chapels, raised over the bodies of Cardinal Beaufort, and Bishop Waynflete. In this part are also several other monuments, slabs, &c. some of which have recently been removed to this from other parts of the Church. The eastern end of the building consists of three distinct Chapels, of which the central, or Virgin Mary Chapel, extends further, and is much larger than the other two: these are small square spaces, separated from the ailes by carved wooden screens, as is also the lady chapel. That on the south has a large altar tomb in the centre, some finely carved wainscotting, with a seat on two sides, and remains of an altar table, &c. at the east end. The wood work of this, as well as of the lady chapel, is elaborately carved, and charged with shields of arms, mottoes, figures, foliage, &c. At the eastern extremities of the ailes are the two *Stair-Cases*, surmounted by octangular turrets, which have been already justly praised by Mr. Garbett. Beneath the presbytery, ailes, lady chapel, &c. is a series of *Crypts*, consisting of three distinct and varied apartments, two of which are certainly ancient, but the other is of comparatively modern formation. In the more ancient one will be found a corresponding style of design to the transepts, in its columns and arches, but varied in proportions, as better adapted to their peculiarity of situation and object. Here the architect formed his plans for posterity : he laid his foundations broad and solid; and directed his works to be plain and firm. The columns, piers, and walls are composed of solid masonry, without the least ornamental sculpture, or moulding.

Having thus briefly pointed out the chief beauties and features of the Church, it is a duty I owe the reader, conformably to the plan adopted in the histories of the other Cathedrals, to notice some of the prominent *deficiencies* and *blemishes* of the present fabric. I regret to say, that these are numerous, although much has been recently done to remove them : and it is hoped, that the same spirit, which impelled the late improvements, may influence the guardians of the Church to prosecute their laudable work with zeal and with judgment[3].

Externally, the whole Church may be completely insulated and easily laid open to public view: the ground on the west and north sides, has accumulated four or five feet, and this should be removed : a lofty wall, at the north-east end, might also be taken away ; other walls on the south side, with a sloping roof, and some extraneous building against the transept, likewise detract from the effect and beauty of that side of the edifice. The whole of this transept requires some essential repairs and restorations, in the masonry and the windows ; and the trifling bell turret, at the angle, should be immediately taken down. The *Tower* has generally been censured as low, flat, and mean ; and with much truth : but it must be

[3] Within the last eight years the present Dean and Chapter have made the following repairs and improvements to the Church :—new roofed the ailes, north and south of the presbytery, and of the Lady Chapel; repaired and new leaded some other parts of the roof; renewed the mullions of the four windows on the south side of the presbytery, and two of those in the south aile ; the great east window, and several windows of the nave, have been carefully repaired ; the finial tabernacles and statues at the east and west ends, and two of the flying buttresses at the south side, have been restored. The north transept has been recently cleaned, pointed, and repaired ; some tombs from the floor of the nave and transepts have been removed to the east end ; the galleries have been cleared, and much white-washing, &c. has been cleaned away. Most of these repairs and alterations are truly judicious and praise-worthy : but some of them, I am sorry to remark, will not justify approbation. The members of the chapter will act wisely to bear in mind, that an English Cathedral may be regarded as national property,—as a public edifice confided to their guardianship, in trust for the whole kingdom. Its founders and successive benefactors thus considered it, and endowed it with repairing funds, to uphold its walls, and support its integral features. Hence it is as much the bounden duty of every succeeding Chapter to guard the fabric from decay, and every species of injury, as it is to attend to the prescribed routine of clerical discipline. Every neglect on their part, and every careless or intentional innovation on the genuine character of the building, is both a dereliction of duty, and an offence to the public. The apathy or wantonness of former officers, will not justify the smallest neglect from those of the present age ; for now the architecture, and each part of these edifices, are regarded with admiration by men of taste ; and the enlightened part of the public, as they must view them with increasing interest, will also watch them with jealousy.

recollected, that this is in unison with the norman part of the Church, and that we examine and admire it more as an architectural specimen of ancient art, than for its beauty of form, or picturesque features. The long and flat extent of the nave and aile, on the south side, presents a dull, monotonous aspect, but this part was formerly provided with an extensive range of cloisters, and some monastic buildings.

Internally, we shall perceive several objects to offend the eye of taste, and many things out of place and out of harmony. Commencing with the Nave and its ailes, there are several marble slabs and monuments inserted in and attached to the walls ; and which are not only injurious to the effect of the whole, but some are destructive of the architecture[*]. In this part we are really surprised to find that the distinguished architectonic prelate, who built the nave, &c., should have placed his own monumental Chantry in a spot to injure the beauty and symmetry of his design. Its screen, instead of harmonizing with the style of the bold clustered columns, to which it is attached, presents a series of tall, meagre mullions, without beauty, and devoid of meaning. Besides, the whole breaks in on the line and massiveness of the nave, interrupts the eye, and attracts the attention to small, and not elegant parts, when it should be fully and wholly occupied by the whole. The architect's best monument

---

[*] It is much to be regretted that our venerable and noble Cathedrals should, for so many ages, have been disgraced and disfigured by petty and pretty monumental tablets. The white, black, and variegated colours, of which they are formed, are not only inimical to all harmony and beauty; but the manner in which they are usually inserted in the walls and columns, is ruinous to the stability of buildings. If the proper officers of the church are regardless of such shameless proceedings, there should be committees of taste, or a general public surveyor appointed, to watch over and direct all the monumental erections, as well as the reparations of each edifice. It is a lamentable fact, that we scarcely ever see a new monument raised with any analogy, or regard to the building in which it is placed. The sculptor and director seem only ostentatious of themselves. To render it showy, imposing, and even obtrusive, is their chief solicitude; and the trustees of a Cathedral are too generally regardless of every thing but handsome fees. Hence Westminster Abbey Church, and Bath Abbey Church, are become mere show rooms of sculpture, and warehouses of marble. A monument recently raised in Salisbury Cathedral, from a design by the Rev. Hugh Owen, is a most praise-worthy exception to this practice. It is also a fine precedent, and amply justifies my anticipation in the history of that Cathedral, *p.* 101.

is his own works, and if these are not calculated to perpetuate and dignify his name, it will never be done by a solitary and more perishable tomb. Wykeham's chantry and tomb are, however, full of beauty and propriety, when compared with some other objects, which we proceed to notice. The Screen, between the nave and choir, said to have been designed by Inigo Jones, is a bad and an unsightly object. It may be said to be in the grecian, or roman, style : indeed it may be pronounced any thing, but in place and in harmony. It is discordant, and highly displeasing, and betrays a deplorable want of feeling in the person, or persons, who designed it for the station, and in those who have sanctioned its continuance for so many years. In niches are two bronze figures, of kings in armour, which do not improve the effect, or appropriation of this offensive screen. Attached to two piers of the nave, on the steps to the choir, are marble monuments to Bishop Hoadley, and to Dr. Joseph Warton : these are most injudiciously placed, are glaringly white, and in their designs present a compound of english, grecian, and emblematic parts, which must detract from the national and simple beauty of a monument. In the north transept we find the pure norman windows, enlarged and altered, their sills lowered, and their openings filled with mullions and tracery :—the west aile is inclosed by a wall, which reaches to the top of the arches :—the timber roof is exposed, and some curious old paintings on the walls are covered with white-wash. The south Transept is also open to the roof, which, with parts of the walls, appear much decayed and dilapidated : and the whole aile is shut out by walls and screens. On entering the Choir the stranger finds some very fine parts, but also some things at war with propriety. The Organ is raised in a gallery beneath the northern arch of the tower, and is thus out of place; its form and fitting up are not calculated to adorn it : and the filling in of the two lofty arches of the tower is injudicious. A wooden ceiling, painted and carved, is thrown across between the four arches of the tower, whereby the lanthorn, or first story of that part of the edifice, is shut out from the floor. This absurd innovation was made in the time of King Charles I. and probably executed chiefly at his expense, as well as the fitting up of the organ. The romanized Bishop's throne; and the canopy, and sham urns, affixed to the

Pl. I.

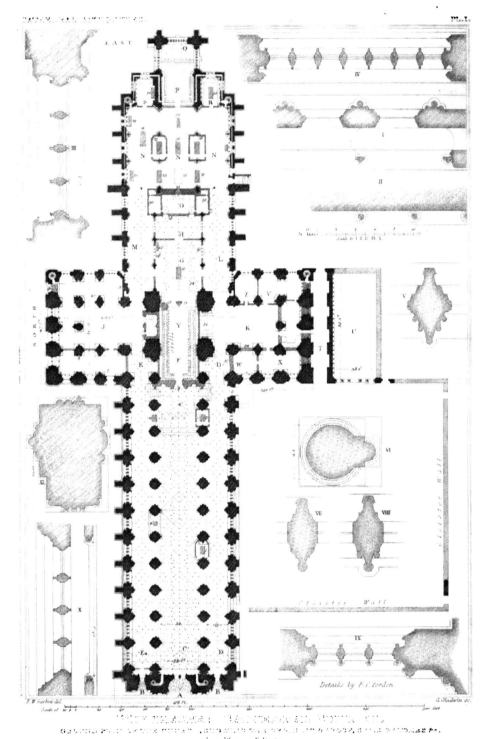

EAST

NORTH

Cloister Wall

Cloister Wall

Details by F. C. Penrose.

also Plans of Parts.

... green, are all of th... ... ... times ... ...
... ... to the pla... ... ... that they are ... ...
... ..., &c. and that ... ... with ...
... coats of white-wash, ... but ... ...
ments should have ... ... that they were not
tolerated ... ...
over the table, and designed ... ...
ever with brown paint, ...
if that was not ... ... it is also ... ...
amidst all this ... ...
Lazarus.” This painting is ... ...
colours, and ... ...
frivolous ... ...
at most ... ...
attitudes; the decora... ... ...
markable for ... ... beauty ... ... In ... ...
altar-screen has been remarked on, as ... ...
for had it been lower, it would ... ...
into the eastern end of the Church and at the ... ...
The effigy of *Beaufort* is a ... ...
worse than its near neighbour ... ...
otherwise account for the extreme ... ... the st... ... supposing that it was placed there at a time ... ... of the
chantry; indeed since the Reformation ... ...
of a stone-mason than of a sculptor ... the effigies of Wykeham ... ...
Edington, de Foix, &c. have all been much mutilated and improved ... to
seek in vain among them for either good expression or perfect face...

PLATE 1.—*Ground Plan* of the whole Church; the darkest shade ... ...
the form and extent of the walls of the present edifice, the lighter ... ...
the south side denotes the direction of the destroyed walls of the chapter-
house and cloister, and the other light tints, within the Church, point out
the sites of tombs, stalls, and screens; whilst the ... of some windows.
... ...

altar-screen, are all of the same tasteless character and times. They are anomalies to the place, and when it is known that they are painted, gilt, varnished, &c. and that the exquisite altar-screen is surcharged with repeated coats of white-wash, we are astonished that such barbarous disfigurements should have remained for nearly two centuries, and that they are still tolerated. Gilpin calls the modern canopy " a sort of penthouse hanging over the table and adorned with festoons of flowers. This is daubed all over with brown paint, totally at variance with every thing around, and as if that was not enough, it is also adorned with profuse gilding. Enshrined amidst all this absurdity, hangs West's Picture of the Resurrection of Lazarus." This painting is censured by the same writer, as to composition, colouring, and management; and Dr. Milner reprobates it on other, but very frivolous grounds. He says, " the apostles here are mere ordinary men, or at most thoughtful philosophers, or elegant courtiers, studious of their attitudes; the devout sisters, in the presence of their beloved master, are remarkable for nothing but their beauty and their sorrow." The height of the altar-screen has been remarked on, as a defect; and with strict propriety: for had it been lower, it would have afforded a pleasing view from the choir into the eastern end of the Church, and of the whole of Fox's east window. The effigy of *Beaufort* is a vulgar, clumsy piece of workmanship, even worse than its near neighbour, that of Sir John Clobery. We cannot otherwise account for the extreme badness of this statue, than by supposing that it was placed there at a time much later than the building of the chantry; indeed since the Reformation. It seems rather the workmanship of a stone-mason than of a sculptor. The effigies of Wykeham, Waynflete, Edington, de Foix, &c. have all been much mutilated and injured, and we seek in vain among them for either good expression or perfect faces.

PLATE I.—*Ground Plan* of the whole Church: the darkest shade shows the form and extent of the walls of the present edifice, the lighter colour, on the south side, denotes the direction of the destroyed walls of the chapter-house and cloister, and the other light tints, within the Church, point out the sites of tombs, stalls, and screens; whilst the plans of some windows, and piers, are shown, to a larger scale, on the sides. A. the chief, or central

L

western porch and door-way: B. B. smaller porches of entrance to the north and south ailes of the nave: C. the nave, extending from the western door to the screen of the choir, 6: D the south aile, and E the north aile: F. choir, fitted up with stalls: G. presbytery: H. space named the sanctuary, inclosed for the altar, or communion table: J. north transept, with an aile on three sides, but that on the west is inclosed by a wall: K. south transept, also with a similar aile, all of which is inclosed by a wall and by screens: L. south aile of the presbytery: M. north aile: N. N. N. three ailes, of de Lucy's architecture, the appropriation of which seems unknown, but may now be properly called the chantry ailes: O. a space named the capitular chapel by Dr. Milner, who says, " the magnificent shrine of St. Swithun, of solid silver, gilt, and garnished with precious stones, the gift of King Edgar, used to be kept here; except on the festivals of the saint, when it was exposed to view upon the altar, or before it. It is not unlikely that other shrines were kept in the same place, ranged against the eastern wall, on which may still be seen some painted figures of saints. This chapel is directly behind the high altar, and formerly communicated with the sanctuary by two doors, which are there still seen: it is, notwithstanding, a two-fold error in our domestic writers to term this place the *Sanctum Sanctorum*, and to describe it as the place from which the priest was accustomed to approach the high altar[5], which is to confound it with the sacristy, or vestry. It was certainly furnished with an altar, the back screen of which, consisting probably of ornamented wood work, seems to have been fastened by certain staples, which still remain. We are assured of this fact, from the circumstance of the early conventual mass, immediately after the holding of a chapter, being celebrated here every morning; from which circumstance it may be called the capitular chapel[6]." P. the Lady, or Virgin Mary Chapel, consisting of two divisions, of two styles of architecture, [see Pl. xx.] with fine carved seats, a rood-loft screen, &c.: Q. altar end of the

---

[5] " Warton's description, *p.* 75, Anonymous History, *vol.* i. *p.* 41. The Greeks indeed, as we have seen, called the altar by the name of ἅγιον ἁγίων; but there is no such name as Sanctum Sanctorum in the whole Latin Liturgy."

[6] Milner's His. Win. ii. 58. Hist. Maj. *l.* iii. *ch.* vi.

same, raised on steps: R. Bishop Langton's monumental chapel, having a large altar tomb in the centre, with seats and highly ornamented screens on the north and south, an open screen with folding doors on the west, and niches, with parts of an altar, to the east: S. a chapel, corresponding in size, and situation, to the former, called the Guardian Angels, or Portland Chapel. This is much altered from its original fitting up, being now occupied by a strange and incongruous medley of tombs, slabs, &c. It is supposed to have acquired its appellation of Guardian Angels, from figures of angels, or cherubs, painted on the ceiling; and latterly the name of Portland, from a stately monument erected against its southern wall to the memory of *Richard Weston, Earl of Portland*, who was Lord Treasurer to King Charles the First. His statue, in bronze, reclines on the tomb, which is further adorned with busts, &c. Against the north wall is a marble slab commemorative of *Bishop Mews*, who, with the above-named nobleman, lie interred in a vault beneath. This chantry is supposed to have been first occupied by the remains of Bishop *Orlton*, who died in 1333, and according to Richardson, in his Notes to Godwin, was interred " in capella propria." In the north wall of this chantry is a large ambre, and in the eastern wall is inserted, but very injudiciously, the side stone of the tomb represented in Plate xxvi. c, whilst the effigy belonging to the same tomb is stationed in another place: T. an arched passage called the *slype*, which formerly communicated from the cloister to the eastern end of the Church; having the *Chapter-house*, U, on the south. The form, extent, and architecture of this apartment are clearly to be ascertained, by the arches and columns on the north and west sides, and by the remains of foundations on the other sides : V. a portion of the east aile of the south transept, called *Prior Silkstede's Chapel*. The letters T.H.O.M.A.S. and S. are curiously carved on the frieze of the screen; and as the letters M. A. are distinguished from the others, and inclosed within a skein of silk, Dr. Milner says, that they form " a monogram of his patroness, the Blessed Virgin :" W. the treasury, &c.: X. vestry, or modern chapter-room, lately cleansed of white-wash, and newly fitted up: Y. part of the choir, immediately under the central tower, or lanthorn: Z. an inclosed chapel, called the Venerable Chapel, and supposed by Dr. Milner to have been the place of interment of *Bishop Courteney*. It is divided from the central aile by an handsome open screen, the upper part of which is adorned with canopies, crocketed pinnacles, &c. From being "highly ornamented and well secured," Dr. Milner believes that "the blessed sacrament used to be kept there, for the benefit of the sick and for private communion." In this chapel are several flat monumental stones and tablets to the Eyre's, Dingley's, Mompesson's, and other families.

The small figures, or Arabic numerals, refer to monuments and to different members of the church :—1. Wykeham's chantry and tomb: 2. Font: 3. Edington's chantry and tomb: 4. a large altar tomb for Bishop Morley: 5. door-way, from the south side, or eastern walk of the old cloister: 6. entrance door to the choir through a modern screen: 7. old Norman door-way to the west aile of the north transept: 8. a curious piscina, near which some of the capitals of the small columns are sculptured to represent busts of kings and bishops: 9. niche in the wall, for a coffin tomb, probably that of de Foix: 10. the intersecting groin here rests on four sculptured capitals, representing human figures, one of which holds something resembling a common chess-board; in the east wall is a very beautiful niche, resting on a sculptured bracket: 11. an opening has lately been made through the wall at this place to the crypts: 12. brass-eagle reading desk: 13. pulpit: 14. bishop's throne, or stall: 15. a coffin tomb, said to cover the remains of King William Rufus: 16. screens inclosing the presbytery and communion-table, &c. On the frieze of the screens are the letters W. H. and R. W. and H. B. with the date 1525, and the mottoes *sit laus deo*, also *in domino confido*, and *est deo gracia:* 17. altar tomb, supposed to cover the remains of Bishop Pontissara: 18. altar screen and altar table: 19. Bishop Fox's chantry: 20. the chantry of Bishop Gardiner: 21. coffin tomb of Wm. de Basynge, lately removed from the south transept: 22. a large flat stone, measuring about twelve feet by five feet, and which formerly was inlaid with brasses of a figure, also "a scripture," or inscription. "This," observes Dr. Milner,

" is celebrated, not only by the vulgar, but also by learned authors[7], as the monument which covers the remains of the great patron saint of our Cathedral and city, *St. Swithun.* The improbability, however, of this opinion is great and obvious ;" for this saint was first interred in the church-yard, and his remains afterwards transferred, by St. Ethelwold, into the Cathedral, where they were deposited in a shrine, or chest of silver, (adorned with precious stones,) which was given by King Edgar for this express purpose[8]. Besides, in the year 1797, Henry Howard, Esq. and some other gentlemen, obtained permission to open this grave, as well as others in the Cathedral; and in this was found an oak coffin, containing a complete skeleton, inclosed in black serge, " probably a monks cowl," with leather boots, or gaiters, sewed on the legs. Milner thinks this must have been the grave, and these the remains, of Prior Silkstede: but when it is remembered that he appears to have fitted up a chapel in the south transept, and assisted so much in finishing the lady chapel, we are more inclined to look for his place of sepulture in either of those parts of the fabric: 23. lid and parts of a coffin tomb, removed from the north and south transepts : 24. a coffin lid, on a raised slab, from the south transept : 25. entrance to the holy-hole, beneath a very fine screen : 26. chantry, inclosing an altar tomb, for Cardinal Beaufort: 27. ditto of Bishop Waynflete : 28. effigy of a Bishop, removed from another part of the church, and raised on modern masonry: 29. a large monument to some persons of the Mason family : 30. a raised coffin tomb, supposed to enshrine the remains of Bishop de Lucy : 31. altar tomb to the memory of Bishop Langton : 32. monument, with effigy, sculpture, to R. Weston, Earl of Portland : 33. stair-case at the north-east angle of the north aile : 34. a large marble monument, adorned with military and naval trophies, to the memory of Sir Isaac Townsend, knight of the garter, and one of the Lords of the Admiralty, who died in 1731 : 36. effigy of a knight in chain-armour, on a piece of masonry, and brought

---

[7] " Clarendon and Gale's Antiquities, *p.* 30. Warton's Description, *p.* 83. A. Wood also seems to countenance this opinion. Athen. Oxon. Alban Butler also in Lives of Saints, July 13."

[8] See Rudborne, His. Maj. *lib.* ii. *c.* 12, and Will. of Malmsbury.

from another part of the church: 36. wall, with blank arches: and 37. ditto, both represented in Plate xxix. A. and B.

The Roman figures refer to certain parts of the building, drawn by *C. F. Porden*, to a larger scale than shown in the general plan: these parts are thus delineated to afford the critical antiquary and architect correct representations of the mullions and mouldings of the windows, &c. It is from such delineations only that we can attain certain knowledge of styles and dates, and discriminate the progressive and almost imperceptible gradations from one form to another. In the four windows, here laid down, and in the three mullions, there will be seen considerable variation in the mouldings, which would not be so readily perceived in viewing the respective windows. It is from the want of correct plans, elevations, and sections of our ecclesiastical edifices, and from an ignorance of their meaning, that so many irrelevant and conjectural essays have been written on the subject: and until all the minute peculiarities of those buildings are faithfully engraved and published, we shall never have a satisfactory knowledge of ancient architecture. Fig. i. a double window of de Lucy's works, with a pier, or large mullion, between the glazing, clustered, slender columns, and half columns on the outside, a passage, or gallery within, arched over, and shafts of clustered columns on the inside. Beneath the sill of the window is an arcade of trefoil headed arches, ii. springing from single purbeck columns. An interior elevation of one compartment of this style is given in Pl. xx. A. Fig. iii. plan, or horizontal section, of one of Fox's windows in the aile of the presbytery, showing three mullions; (one of which is still further enlarged, Fig. viii.) also the forms of the mouldings, on the sides of the window, &c.: Fig. iv. plan of the eastern window of the lady chapel, having six mullions, (one of which is seen at Fig. vii.) and deep hollow mouldings on each side. One window on the north side, and the other to the south, correspond in form, size, &c. to the eastern. A view of the first is given in Plate viii. and an elevation of that on the north side in Plate xx. C.: Fig. v. mullion of Edington's window: vi. column at the north end of the north transept; that at the opposite extremity of the south transept corresponds: vii. and viii. have been already noticed: ix. plan of one of Wykeham's windows in the áile of the nave: x. plan of one of Fox's windows in the clerestory of the presbytery: xi. plan of the north-east great pier, under the tower.

PLATE II. *Plan and Section of the Crypts, &c.* It is hoped that this plate will prove very interesting to the architectural antiquary ; as the very curious and early part of Winchester Church, laid down in this plan, No. 2. has never before been represented by engraving ; and consequently could not have been fully known to the public. As here defined, its forms, dimensions, and style may be easily understood. It consists of three portions, or distinct parts:—first, the large, or chief crypt, formed of a central apartment, A, having two ailes, with a row of columns: B. B, its ailes, continued round the semi-circular end, C : a second, or smaller crypt, D, with semi-circular end, and divided into two parts by a row of four columns, and a fifth, which is placed in the centre of the entrance, l. From the windows, through the walls of this apartment, it seems very evident that the whole was formed anterior to the substructure of de Lucy's work, marked by the buttresses p. p. p. ; and from the style of the columns and arches, I cannot persuade myself to believe that it is anterior to the larger crypt, the chapter-house, or the transepts. At m. n. the wall is broken away to open a communication with the third crypt, E, the vaulting of which rests on two columns: one of these is represented, 5 : on the south side are two windows, two others at the east end, and one on the north side, where there is also a door-way. The smaller letters refer to different parts of those crypts ; a. and b. stair-cases from the ailes of the church : c. door-way from the outside: d. a well : e. door-way from the north side : f. f. f. arched openings from the aile to the centre: g. g. g. small apertures, or windows: h. wall of the transept: i. i. i. buttresses: k. two larger buttresses : l. m. n. already noticed : o. ground beneath the floor of de Lucy's ailes : p. p. p. buttresses to the same: q. vault under the Guardian angels chapel, with two coffins, supposed of Bishop Mews and the Earl of Portland: r. a corresponding space to the former, beneath Langton's chapel, but there is no exterior indication of a vault: s. door-way.—No. 1. shows the section of the three crypts with the floor above: 1. steps to the altar : 2. steps immediately behind the altar screen : and 3. steps to St. Swithun's altar : 4. holy-hole : 5. floor of de Lucy's work : 6. floor of the lady chapel ; and 7. altar end of ditto : 3. column, and 4. pier of the large crypt : 5. column of the eastern crypt ; and 6. capital and base of the central crypt.

PLATE III. *Capitals and Bases.* B. C. of the nave : D. E. of the transept : F. G. of de Lucy's work : and H. I. of the presbytery : K. plan of a pier of the nave, the dark-line of which shows the additional casing and forms of the mouldings made by Wykeham : L. plan of one of the clustered columns in the presbytery, with bases, &c.

PLATE IV. *View of the West Front,* the age and architecture of which have been already noticed by Mr. Garbett, *p.* 64. This is evidently the workmanship of three different eras : 1st. the original walls, with hexangular stair-case turrets, which appear to have been of a very early date, if not really of the age of Walkelyn : 2d. the central large and two lateral windows, with the panelling and tracery on the walls, most likely of Edington's age : and 3d. the three porches with the open parapets, which Mr. Garbett assigns, for the first time, to Cardinal Beaufort.

PLATE V. By *the section and plan* of the west front, the interior elevation of the windows, door-ways, pinnacles, &c. are correctly displayed ; as well as sections of the archivolt mouldings of the windows and arches on the north side : a. elevation of the pier of clustered columns and hollow mouldings : b. section of the opposite pier : c. section of the wall, between the windows, of the arch of the aile, and of the concealed flying buttress from the wall of the nave to that of the aile : d. section of the wall, beneath the window of the north aile : e. western door-way to the north aile : f. window of the clerestory, to the nave, over which is a section of its mouldings and of the parapet : g. section of the window of the north aile, beyond which is shown the profile of the large buttress on the north side, surmounted by a crocketed pinnacle, having a finial : h. a gallery, or floor, raised over the western end of the north aile, now used as the ecclesiastical court, and containing documents belonging to the church, but formerly employed as a *tribune,* according to Dr. Milner, " to contain the extraordinary minstrels, who performed on grand occasions, when some prelate,

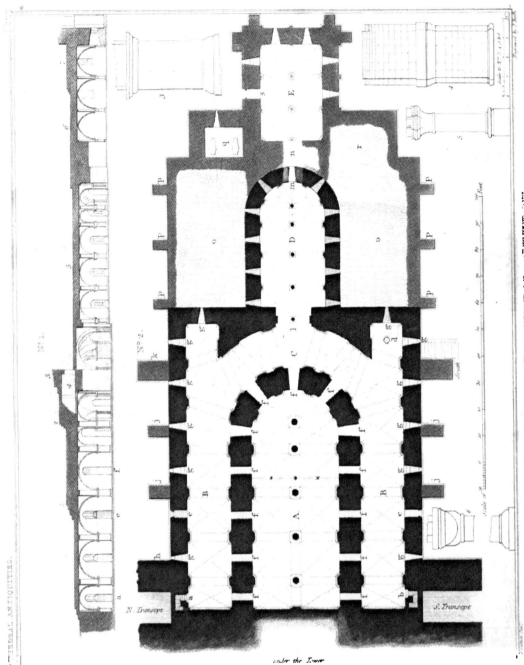

WINCHESTER CATHEDRAL CHURCH.

Plan & Section of the Crypt &c.

London Published March 1 1817 by Longman & Co Paternoster Row.

London Published Oct.1 1822 by Longman & Co. Paternoster Row

Printed by _____ & Barnett

Engraved by Ranson from a Drawing by J. F. Brisden for Britton's History of Winchester Cathedral.

WINCHESTER CATHEDRAL. INTERIOR.

CAPITALS & BASES.

London Published Oct.r 1.1817. by Longman & Co. Paternoster Row.

Printed by Cox & Barnett

Engraved by J. Le Keux, from a Drawing by Edw Blore for Brittons History &c. of Winchester Cathedral.

WINCHESTER CATHEDRAL CHURCH,
View of the West front.

TO THE HONORABLE AND REVEREND AUGUSTUS GEORGE LEGGE, M. A. ARCHDEACON OF WINCHESTER, CHAPLAIN
IN ORDINARY TO HIS MAJESTY &c &c. This Plate is inscribed by the Author.

London, Published May 1, 1817 by Longman &c. Paternoster Row.

WINCHESTER CATHEDRAL CHURCH.

Section & Plan of the West front.

London Published Dec.r 1. 1816. by Longman & C.o Paternoster Row.

Printed by Coe & Barnett.

legate, or king, was received at the Cathedral in solemn state, by a
procession of the whole convent.   At such times the cross-bearers, alco-
lyths, and thurifers, led the way, and the bishop, prior, and other dignified
clergy, in their proper insignia and richest vestments, closed the ranks.
In the mean time the Church was hung from one end to the other with
gorgeous tapestry, representing religious subjects, the large hooks for
supporting which still remain fixed to the great columns; the altars dazzled
the beholders with a profusion of gold, silver, and precious stones, the
lustre of which was heightened by the blaze of a thousand wax lights, whilst
the well-tuned voices of a numerous choir, in chosen psalms and anthems,
gave life and meaning to the various minstrelsy that was performed in this
tribune."   Such was the religious pomp and gorgeous parade of the
possessors of these Cathedrals in former times, as described by one who
has been initiated in the mysteries of monachism, and who partially thinks
the revival of it would be conducive to the happiness of the human race:
i. door-way from the turret stairs to the parapet.

   Plan of the West End. A. recessed porch of entrance to the nave, in which
the forms of the groining to the roof are defined, as well as the panelling of
the sides, and the mullion, or clustered column in the centre of the door-way:
B. southern, and C. northern porches: D. mullions and mouldings to the
western window of the south aile, beneath which was formerly a door: E.
corresponding window on the north side: F. one compartment of the north
aile, showing the number and disposition of the ribs, at the intersection of
each of which is a shield, or large boss: H. south aile ditto.   [The form of
the rib here laid down as an octagon, should have been drawn in a lozenge
or diamond shape, as marked in the centre of the nave, and as indicated
in the general plan.]   G. groining of the nave, the lines on the sides of
which indicate the mouldings of the arches.   The darkest tint, at the west
end, shows the masonry of the three porches, which have evidently been
raised between the turrets and buttresses, and which are denoted, as well as
the mullions of the windows, by a lighter colour.   [For extreme width of
west front read 118 feet, instead of 128 feet.]

M

PLATE VI. *View of the North Transept*, &c. Although much of the original work of this elevation remains, we cannot contemplate without regret that so much alteration and innovation has been adopted. Each of the four bottom windows, as well as those of the second and third stories, have been fitted up with mullions, tracery, and masonry : the two windows over the ailes are wholly closed up ; some masonry, blank arches, &c. have been evidently taken away from the north-eastern angle, as may be inferred from the fragment of an arch seen against the buttress. In the gable is a circular window, with mullions of rather unusual form and character.

PLATE VII. *View of the North Side,* from a place called Paradise, displays several very interesting and varied features and parts of the church : first, on the left hand, is the window and blank arches, belonging to the guardian angels chapel : second, the turret stair-case at the north-east end of de Lucy's work, also the exterior of the windows, buttresses, and parapet of the north aile of the same : third, the enriched eastern gable and window, octangular turrets, flying-buttresses, pinnacles, &c. of Fox's architecture : fourth, the central tower : and fifth, the north transept, with its windows and buttresses. [The foreground of this print does not pretend to represent the local appropriation of the place, which is a kitchen garden belonging to the deanery.]

PLATE VIII. *View of the East End of the Church,* which shows the great eastern window, the panelling beneath, the parapet, corbel table, &c. all supposed to have been built by Silkstede, Hunton, and Courteney : the window with two mullions and tracery, belongs to Langton's chapel.

PLATE IX. *South Transept, &c.* [Here also the artist has very properly omitted the local, but irrelevant objects of culinary plants and garden walls : he has also omitted a tall pan-tile roof, which obscures the four bottom windows of the transept, and has represented the three arches, at the west end of the chapter-house, as open.] This view displays the arcade on the north side of the chapter-house : the whole face of the southern tran-sept, with the peculiar panelling of the gable : also a long extent of the south side of the nave, and its aile : the tower, part of the upper story of the presbytery, and its south aile.

Engraved by J. Le Keux, from a Drawing by Edw. Blore, for Britton's History &c. of Winchester Cathedral.

WINCHESTER CATHEDRAL CHURCH.

View of the North Transept &c.

TO SIR THOMAS BARING BART this Plate is respectfully inscribed by the Author.

London Published March 1 1817, by Longman & Co. Paternoster Row.

Printed by Hayward.

WINCHESTER CATHEDRAL CHURCH.

View of North side of Choir &c. from N.E.

TO THE REV.ᵈ GEORGE FREDERICK NOTT, D.D. F.S.A. Prebendary of Winchester Cathedral &c. this Plate is inscribed by the Author.

London, Published Dec.ʳ 1 1816 by Longman & Cᵒ. Paternoster Row.

Drawn by Edw.d Blore.
Interior History &c. of Winchester Cathedral.
Engraved by R.Sands.

WINCHESTER CATHEDRAL CHURCH,
VIEW OF THE EAST END.
TO THE REV.d HARRY LEE; FELLOW OF WINCHESTER COLLEGE, &c. &c.
This Plate is inscribed by the AUTHOR.

London, Published June 1. 1816 by Longman &c. Paternoster Row.

Printed by Cox & Barnett.

TO THE REV.ᴰ THO.ˢ RENNELL D.D.F.S.A. Dean of Winchester &c &c to the Dean of the Church ... is Inscribed by the Author

London Published Aug.ᵗ 1.181 by Longman & ... Paternoster Row

Printed & Coloured

Engraved by B. Winkles from a Drawing by Edw. Blore for Britton History &c. of Winchester Cathedral.

WINCHESTER CATHEDRAL CHURCH.

NAVE, LOOKING EAST.

To BENJAMIN WINSTON Esq. of Winchester this plate is inscribed from Motives of Friendship by J. Britton.

Engraved by W. Radclyffe after a Drawing by Edw. Blore for Britton's History &c. of Winchester Cathedral.

WINCHESTER CATHEDRAL CHURCH.

To the Revd. Archdeacon Hoare, LL.D. F.R.S. P.S.A. Prebendary of Winchester &c. this Plate is inscribed by the Author.

London, Published Oct. 1. 1816. by Longman. & Co. Paternoster Row.

Printed by Hayward

Engraved by R. Sands from a Drawing by Edw. Blore for Britton's History &c. of Winchester Cathedral

WINCHESTER CATHEDRAL CHURCH.

View of the North Transept, looking N.E.

TO RICHARD POWELL M.D. F.R.S. & A.S. Fellow of the College of Physicians, Physician to St. Bartholomews Hospital, & Vice President of the Society of Arts &c. this Plate is inscribed by the Author.

London Published March 1.1817 by Longman & Co. Paternoster Row.

Printed by Jas R. Barnes

Engraved by W. Radclyffe from a Drawing by Edwd Blore, for Britton's History &c. of Winchester Cathedral.

WINCHESTER CATHEDRAL CHURCH,
CHOIR, LOOKING WEST.

To the REVd THOs SILVER, D.C.L. Professor of Poetry, in the University of Oxford, &c &c. This plate is
Inscribed by the Author.

London, Published Jan 1, 1818, by Longman & Co Paternoster Row.

and may be soon removed, it was deemed advisable to omit it in the view. From the same feelings, the draftsman has left out the Bishop's stall, which is attached to the left hand pier, and also a boarded partition, which fills up the whole of the southern arch under the tower.]

PLATE XIV. Part of the *Stalls* of the Choir. The design and carving of these seats present abundant studies for the professional and amateur artists. The compartments here represented are the central entrance doorway to the choir, and three stalls on each side, with their respective moveable seats, or *misereres*[9]. At the back of the seats is a series of arcades, highly ornamented with tracery and carvings, and each seat is surmounted by a tall, narrow canopy, splendidly enriched with crockets, finials, cusps, and other ornaments. From the style of the arches and decorations of these stalls, they have been generally attributed to Edington's prelacy and munificence. In the inner mouldings of the three western door-ways, we recognise the same style and similar cusps.

PLATE XV. *View of the Altar Screen.* Among the architectural beauties of this, and of any other cathedral, there will not perhaps be found one to excel that represented in the annexed print. Niches of various sizes and situations, pedestals, canopies, and pilaster-buttresses, cover nearly the whole face of this sumptuous design; whilst its upper division and summit is crowded to excess with pierced work, crocketed pinnacles, and perforated canopies. In the centre is a projecting canopy, most elaborately executed; but its appropriate pedestal is lost: as are also several other parts belonging to the middle and lower part of the screen. The accompanying print shows it as it would appear if divested of the tasteless urns, in the niches, and of the carved wood work, now before it. The screen is executed in a fine white, soft stone, but is thickly covered and obscured by

___

[9] Dr. Milner's account of these seats, if not improbable, is calculated to render some of the monastic discipline very ridiculous. He states, that the misereres were formed to expose and punish sleepy monks : " on these," he relates, " the monks and canons of ancient times, with the assistance of their elbows, on the upper part of their stalls, half supported themselves during certain parts of their long offices, not to be obliged always to stand or kneel. This stool, however, was so contrived, that if the body became supine by sleep, it naturally fell down, and the person who rested upon it was thrown forward into the middle of the choir."

.

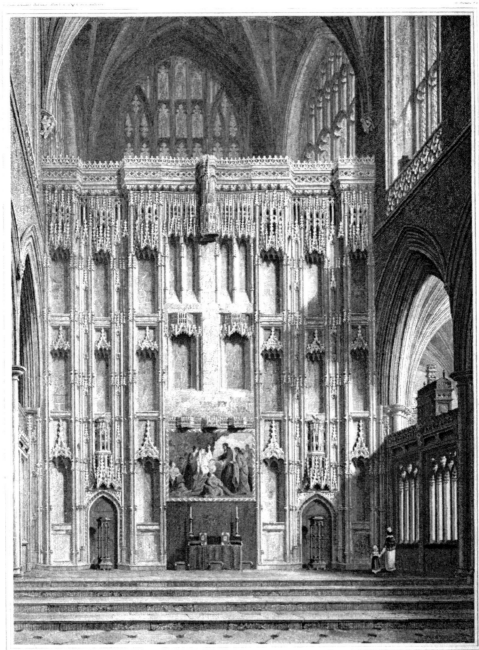

Engraved by F. Le Keux from a Drawing by Edw. Blore for Britton's History &c. of Winchester Cathedral

WINCHESTER CATHEDRAL CHURCH.

VIEW OF THE HIGH ALTAR.

TO THE REV.D EDMUND POULTER M.A. Prebendary of Winchester and Chaplain to the Lord Bishop of the diocess,
This Plate is inscribed by the Author

London, Published July 1 1817 by Longman & C.º Paternoster Row.

Printed by Dawson.

WINCHESTER CATHEDRAL CHURCH.
VIEW OF WYKEHAM'S CHANTRY &c.

To the WARDEN & FELLOWS of NEW COLLEGE OXFORD; and to the WARDEN & FELLOWS of WINCHESTER COLLEGE.
the Guardians & Preservers of the above Chantry, this view of it is inscribed by J.Britton.

London, Published June 1.1817 by Longman & C.º Paternoster Row

white-wash. In the spandrils of the two side-doors are sculptured representations, in basso-relievo, of the Annunciation and Visitation, but executed in a very bad style. With its original altar, and Catholic embellishments, this screen must have been magnificently rich and splendid. Its furniture, &c. are thus described by Dr. Milner, from an inventory printed in the Monasticon, from the report of the commissioners in the time of Henry the Eighth: " The nether part, or antependium of the high altar, consisted of plated gold, garnished with precious stones. Upon it stood the tabernacle and steps, of embroidered work, ornamented with pearls, as also six silver candlesticks, gilt, intermixed with reliquaries, wrought in gold and jewels. Behind these was a table of small images, standing in their respective niches, made of silver, adorned with gold and precious stones. Still higher was seen a large crucifix with its attendant images, viz. those of the Blessed Virgin and St. John, composed of the purest gold, garnished with jewels, the gift of Bishop Henry de Blois, King Stephen's brother. Over this appears to have been suspended from the exquisite stone canopy, the crown of King Canute, which he placed there, in homage to the Lord of the Universe, after his famous scene of his commanding the sea to retire from his feet, which took place at Southampton[10]." Mr. Garbett, in *p.* 66, ascribes the erection of the altar-screen to Cardinal Beaufort, but I am rather inclined to attribute it to Bishop Waynflete, who had, previous to his death, constructed his own monumental chantry; and to the workmanship and materials of which it so nearly corresponds.

PLATE XVI. View of *Wykeham's Chantry*, from the nave, shows the northern entrance door-way, with two niches, canopies, and pedestals over it, the whole of the screen towards the nave, the enriched niches at the east end, with parts of the architecture of the nave. Within the screen is an altar tomb, in the centre, sustaining the effigy of the prelate, repre-

---

[10] The altar-screen, in St. Alban's Abbey Church, has generally been compared to this at Winchester; but although its general form, and some of its niches, are similar, the whole is very different, and much less elaborate in detail. It was built by Abbot Wallingford, about 1482, and cost 1100 marks. See Clutterbuck's History of Hertfordshire, *vol.* i. *p.* 35, in which work is a finely engraved view of the screen by Mr. H. Le Keux.

sented in pontificalibus, with small statues of three monks kneeling at his feet. [See Plate xxv. B.] The altar tomb is of white marble, with canopied niches at the sides and ends; and at present is disfigured, as well as the statue, by crude colours and gilding[11]. At the head of the monument, attached to the pier of the nave, are five tabernacles, or niches : at the east end are marks of the altar, with the credence table at the right hand, and a piscina.

PLATE XVII. View of the *Chantries of Beaufort, Waynflete, &c.* The combination of objects, represented in this plate, has been already noticed, *p.* 75, and their names and situations, in *p.* 85. The first object on the left hand is part of *Fox's Chantry*, a. which consists of a screen, the lower portion of which is inclosed, filled up within, and ornamented on the outside with a series of niches, with pedestals and canopies, also with octangular panelled buttresses at the angles, and panels between each niche. Its southern side, or principal front, may be described to be composed of three divisions, in height, and four in length. Each of the latter displays an ornamented, perforated parapet and frieze, with a small pedestal rising in the centre, supporting the figure of a pelican, Fox's crest. Beneath the frieze is a double window, with mullions and tracery, ornamented with crockets, finials, and embattled mouldings. Under this window is a double line, or facia, of sculpture, beneath which is the series of niches, &c. already described. In the second compartment, from the east, is a recess, containing the effigy of an emaciated human figure, with the feet resting against a skull, and the head on a mitre. Thus, instead of representing his own person, and features, the prelate thought it more consistent with christian humility to exhibit this mortifying lesson to man; to show the nothingness of his body when deprived of the animating spirit; and intimating that pride and arrogance are petty vanities, unworthy of man and degrading to his nature.

---

[11] The College of Winchester, and that of New College, Oxford, have latterly contributed to preserve and embellish this tomb and chantry. According to Dr. Milner, it was first " repaired and ornamented soon after the Restoration, viz. in 1664, and again in 1741, but with very little judgment, as to the distinguishing and colouring of the several ornaments." It was again painted, gilt, &c. by Mr. Cave, of Winchester, in 1797.

It is rather curious that there is neither tomb, statue nor inscription to commemorate the founder of this sumptuous chantry. In the western compartment is a finely carved door. [See PLATE XXI.] The interior is
" luxuriantly," as Milner says, ornamented with tabernacles, sculpture, and
architectural enrichments. It is divided into three parts, by a raised floor,
and by a screen with a door-way. East of the latter is a little vestry,
which still contain the ambries. The wall over the altar is decorated with
three large, and sixteen small niches; also a facia of demi-angels, shields,
&c. The ceiling is adorned with tracery and shields of the royal arms of
the house of Tudor, emblazoned with colours and gilding. In the vestry,
over the ambries, is a niche, corresponding with those over the holy-hole;
and implying that the screen was formerly adorned with two rows of those
enriched niches. The windows of this chantry appear to have been
formerly glazed with painted glass[12]. Waynflete's chantry, b. will be
noticed in the next plate. *Beaufort's Chantry,* c. consists of clustered
piers, with a panelled screen at the base, an open screen at the head, or
west end, and a closed screen at the east end. There are doors on the
north and south sides, and the whole is surmounted by a mass of canopies,
niches, and pinnacles, which bewilder the sight and senses, by their number and complexity. Beneath this gorgeous canopy is an altar tomb, in
the centre of the inclosure, with the statue, already noticed and criticised.
Milner says, " that the figure represents Beaufort in the proper dress of a
Cardinal : viz. the scarlet coat and hat, with long depending cords, ending
in tassels of ten knots each. The low balustrade and tomb, the latter of
which is lined with copper, and was formerly adorned on the outside with
the arms of the deceased, enchased on shields, are of grey marble. The
pious tenor of his will, which was signed two days before his death, and
the placid frame of his features, in the figure before us, which is probably a
portrait, leads us to discredit the fictions of poets and painters, who describe

---

[12] A long dissertation by Mr. Gough, with very inaccurate plates of this chantry, from drawings
by J. Schnebbelie, have been published in the second volume of the " Vetusta Monumenta."

him as dying in despair[13]." After what has been said, *p. 81*, of this statue, it will be unnecessary to offer another remark.

Langton's Chantry, e. has been already noticed, p. 77 and 83. Its elaborately carved screen, with folding doors, and open gallery, or rood-loft, are shown in this print : also a view into the lady chapel under, d. One compartment of the carved wainscotting round this chapel is delineated in Pl. xxi.

PLATE XVIII. *View of the Chantries* of *Waynflete*, Beaufort, and Gardiner, with parts of de Lucy's, Fox's, and Walkelyn's architecture. The principal chantry in this view, presents a gorgeous mass of architectural and sculptural ornaments : in which the designer appears to have exerted his fancy to combine, in one object, and in a small compass, an almost countless assemblage of pinnacles, canopies, niches, and sculptured details. The interior, as well as the exterior, is covered with decorative work : its two ends are filled with tabernacles, and its inner roof covered with a profusion of tracery, arranged in various elegant forms. [See Plate xix.] From the multiplicity of parts in this single chantry, it would be tedious to describe the whole. Aided by the view, plan, and statue, the stranger may form a tolerably accurate opinion of its style, form, and decoration. Chandler, in his Life of Waynflete, says he could not find any " particular information" concerning this " chapel of St. Mary Magdalen ;" whence he infers, that it was executed during the life-time of the prelate, and was also " furnished with missals, copes, and other requisites." The material of Waynflete's chantry, is a fine, soft, white stone ; easily worked by the mason's and sculptor's tools : and its chief parts and ornaments are still in good preservation. The *Chantry* to *Bishop Gardiner*, seen beyond that of Waynflete, forms a curious contrast to the latter, and also to its corresponding chantry, that for Fox. As the vast power and tyranny of the Catholic

---

[13] " Shakespeare and Sir Joshua Reynolds ; the former in his Henry VI.—the latter in a celebrated picture." The former, most probably, derived his opinions of the prelate from the English Chronicles, (See Holinshed's, iii. 212, 4to. 1808.) his chief sources for historical character ; and the latter merely illustrated, by a painting, a passage of the poet. The language of the bard, in portraying the haughty Cardinal, is pointedly strong and descriptive.

CATHEDRAL ANTIQUITIES.

a   b   c   d   e

Engraved by Edw.d Turrell, from a Drawing by Edw.d Blore, for Britton's History of Winchester Cathedral.

WINCHESTER CATHEDRAL CHURCH.

BEAUFORT CHANTRY, WITH PART OF FOX'S, WAYNFLETE'S, AND LANGTON'S CHANTRIES.

TO THE REV.d J. INGRAM, M.A. Fellow of Trinity College, Oxford, and author of a Lecture on Anglo-Saxon Literature &c.

This Plate is inscribed from motives of long friendship & esteem, by J. Britton.

London, Published Sep.t 1 1818, by Longman & C.o Paternoster Row

WAYNFLETE'S CHANTRY, WITH THOSE FOR CHANCELLOR & BEAUFORT.

WINCHESTER CATHEDRAL CHURCH.

TO THE PRESIDENT & FELLOWS OF S.t MARY MAGDALEN COLLEGE, OXFORD, the patrons & preservers of Waynflete's splendid Monumental Chantry,

This Plate is inscribed by J. Britton.

London. Published, Sep. 1, 1817, by Longman & C.o Paternoster Row.

East

WINCHESTER CATHEDRAL CHURCH.

Groined Roof to Wykeham's Chantry, & Plan of Clustered Columns H H

London Published June 1 1817 by Longman & C. Paternoster Row

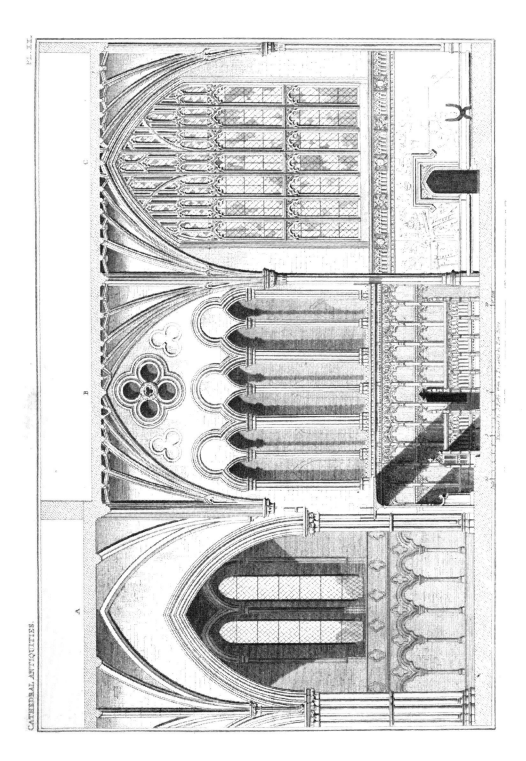

church, had experienced a severe shock, in the life-time of Gardiner, so the ecclesiastical architecture of the country was also revolutionized. Its decline is strikingly marked in this Bishop's chantry; where we see a compound mixture of bad Italian and bad English; the lower part representing the former, and the upper part the latter.

PLATE XIX. *Groined Roof to Waynflete's Chantry.* This print displays not only the forms and ornaments of the ceiling of this splendid chantry, but likewise the horizontal sections of the screens, buttresses, and mullions; also the clustered columns of de Lucy's architecture: A. A. door-ways: B. B. clustered columns, with detached shafts of purbeck marble: a. seat, or plinth, round the screen: b. b. buttresses: c. c. mullions: d. d. niches, or tabernacles.

PLATE XX. Elevation of *Three Compartments;* two on the north side *of the Lady Chapel*, B. C. and one of de Lucy's architecture, A. In the spandrils of the door-way of the eastern compartment, is some sculpture of foliage, entwining an ornamental T. on one side, and the letter N. in a tun or barrel, on the other side, being the initial letter for Thomas, and the rebus for Hunton, Henton, or N-ton, one of the priors. This door-way is supposed to have opened to a sextry, on the north side. In this part is still kept the remnant of a Chair, which was handsomely ornamented with velvet, enamelling, &c. Gale says, that it was used at, if not made for, the royal marriage between Queen Mary and Philip of Spain. The lower walls of this chapel were formerly covered with a series of fresco paintings, which from neglect and wanton mischievousness, are nearly obliterated. Carter, in his "Specimens of Ancient Sculpture and Painting," has published four etchings of the different subjects, and Dr. Milner has endeavoured to elucidate them by a long dissertation. The whole vaulting of this chapel appears to have been executed by Priors Hunton and Silkstede, whose names are painted on the roof; the latter connected with a figure of a horse, or steed. The groins, or ribs, rest on very elegant capitals. The stalls and wainscotting, as well as the rood-screen of this chapel, are highly charged with rich carving; one compartment of which is delineated in Pl. XXI.

N

PLATE XXI. Specimens of *Carved Wood-work*, from the Lady Chapel, Langton's chapel, Fox's chantry, and the pulpit; all of which are so finely executed, that it is hoped the Dean and Chapter will not suffer any further dilapidation or destruction in these interesting remains of former times.

PLATE XXII. Part of the *Altar Screen*, being the east side of one of the door-ways, with canopies over it. In the spandrils are two slips of foliage very finely executed, which, with the canopies, have a close resemblance to the style of Waynflete's chantry.—The central *niche* of an *old screen* behind the altar, facing the east, which I am inclined to think was executed at the latter end of Edward the First's, or beginning of the Second Edward's reign. This screen presents nine of these niches, besides one which is inclosed in Fox's chantry. From the unusual situation of the screen, I am induced to think, that it was originally placed on the opposite side of the wall, with its niches facing the west, and forming the altar screen. The crockets, finials, and various foliage of the pediments and pinnacles of these niches, are elaborately wrought; as well as a sculptured frieze beneath the pedestals. Every niche appears to have contained two pedestals, under each of which is still one of the following names:—DOMINVS JESVS:—Sᶜᵃ MARIA:—KYNGILSVS REX:—Sᵉˢ BIRINUS EPC.:—KYNWALDUS REX:—EGBERTUS REX.—ADULFUS REX FILI EJ:—EGBERTUS REX:—ELURED REX FILI EJ:—EDWARD. REX SENIOR:—ATHELSTAN. REX FILI EJ:—EDRADUS REX:—EDGAR REX:—EMMÆ REGINA:—ALWINUS EPIS:—ETHELRED. REX: Sᵉˢ EDWARD. REX FILI EJ:—CNUTUS REX:—HARDICNUT. REX FILIUS EJUS. Most of the above personages were interred in Winchester, and all but two were benefactors to the Cathedral.—A small part of *Fox's Chantry* displays the style of the turrets, the elegant parapet, the frieze, two canopies, and part of the tracery of one window.

PLATE XXIII. Section of *de Lucy's Three Ailes*, east of the altar, &c. Among the architectural plates that have been engraved for the publications of the Society of Antiquaries, and for other works, I believe it may be confidently stated that no one presents such a combination and variety of parts,

Lady Chapel

Langtons Chapel

Door to Foxes Chantry

Pulpit

Engraved by Edwd. Purcell after a Drawing by Edw. Blore.

WINCHESTER CATHEDRAL CHURCH.

Carved Wood Work

London Published May 1 1817 by Longman & Co Paternoster Row.

Printed by Chas B. Harwood.

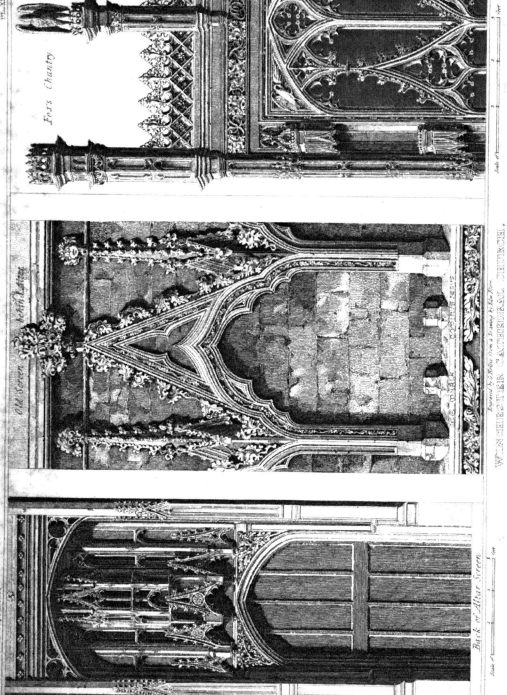

CATHEDRAL ANTIQUITIES.

PL. XXXII.

Back of Altar Screen.

Old Screen. *Archin Paning.*

Fox's Chantry

Engraved by J. Roffe from a Drawing by Edw. Blore.

WINCHESTER CATHEDRAL CHURCH.

Parts of Altar Screen — Old Screen — & Fox's Chantry.

London, Published May 1 1817, by Longman & Co. Paternoster Row.

Engraved by John Le Keux from a drawing by Edw. Blore for Britton's History &c. of Winchester Cathedral.

WINCHESTER CATHEDRAL CHURCH,

SECTION & ELEVATION EAST ON THE ALTAR SCREEN.

TO THE REV.d FREDERIC IREMONGER A.M. F.L.S. Author of Sermons & Essays on the reformation of Criminals
& education of poor children &c.   This plate is Inscribed by J. Britton.

London, Published Aug.t 1 1817 by Longman & Co. Paternoster Row.

London by Barnard.

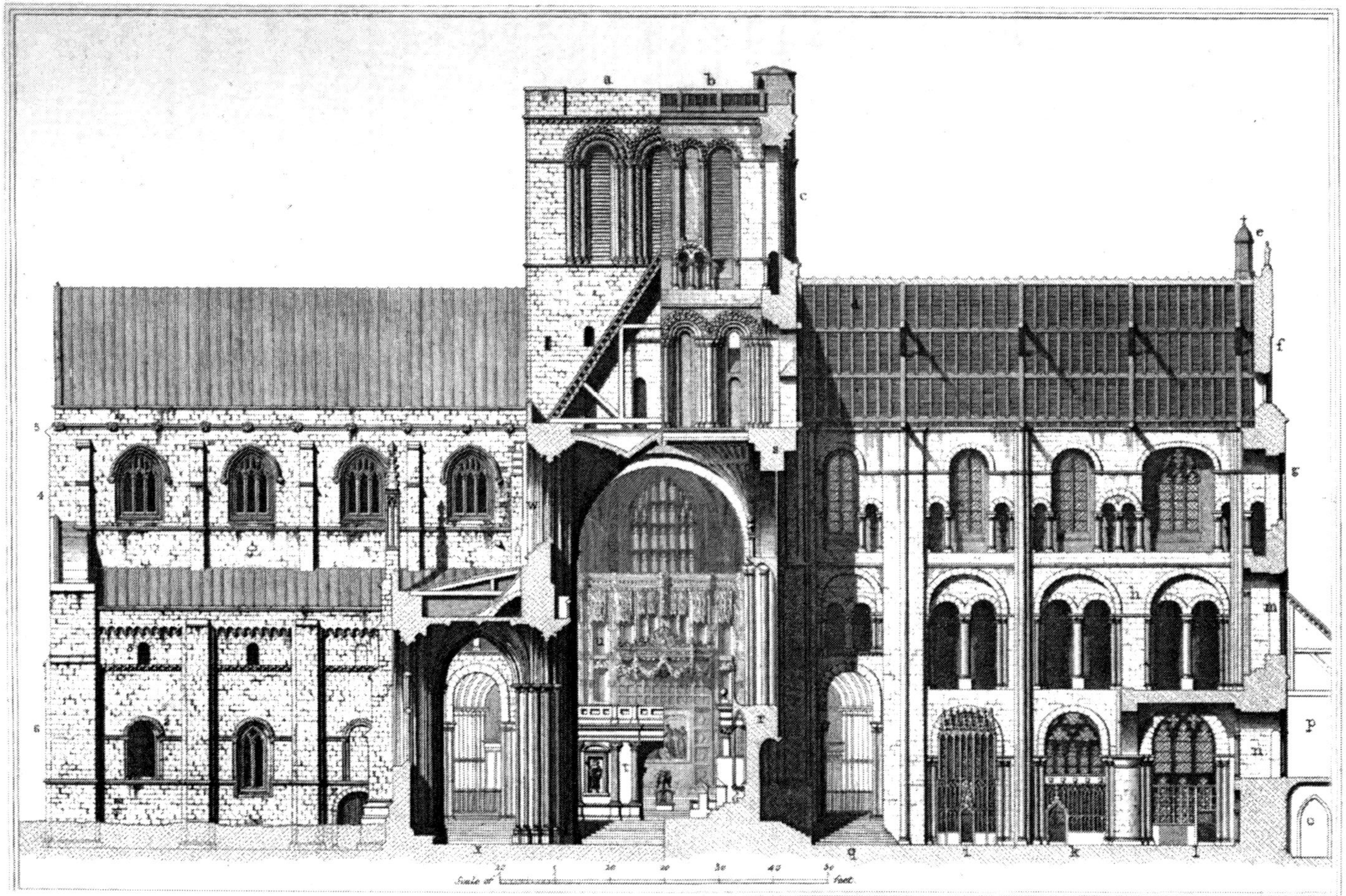
a
b
c
e
f
g
h
i
k
l
m
n
o
p
q
r
s
t
w
x
Scale of 10 1 10 20 30 40 50 Feet

styles, and objects, as that now under consideration. Here we are presented with elevations of arches, columns, windows, &c. of distinct and distant ages; from the middle of the eleventh century to the middle of the sixteenth: the crypt, transepts, and tower display the former, whilst the latter is contained in the chantry of Gardiner, i. The small letters refer to the principal objects:—a. a. outer aile of the crypt, showing the bases of the columns and piers : b. b. two inner ailes, divided by columns, d : c. section of piers : e. elevation of one of the openings, with section of the arch above : f. section through one of the windows : g. holy-hole, beneath the old altar screen : h. east end of Fox's chantry : i. ditto of Gardiner's : k. section of the south wall of de Lucy's work, representing the gallery, or passage through the wall ; on the inside is an insulated purbeck column, supporting the rib of the vault : l. clustered columns of detached shafts of purbeck marble : m. section of the opposite cluster, with the wall above : n. two arches, springing from clustered columns, having their bases on a high wall, and which, as already remarked, I conjecture was the former place of the altar-screen, before the present lofty one was erected, the back of which is seen through the two arches : o. section of the timber work of the roof: the latter is singularly wide and flat: p. profile elevation of one of the large buttresses, which receives the flying abutment from the S. E. angle, u : q. upper division of the east aile of the south transept, showing one of the small windows to the triforium : r. filled arch in the wall over the aile, above which, at s. are the clerestory windows of the transept : t. corbel table, which extends all round the transepts. The central acute gable, with crockets, panelling, octangular turrets, window, &c. display the florid style and workmanship of Fox's architecture. The narrow, tall openings, with horse-shoe arches, are the most eastern remnants of Walkelyn's works; and the parts of windows and doors seen through them are those at the western end, which do not range in straight lines with the ailes of the presbytery.

PLATE XXIV. *Half Elevation and Half Section of the Church*, from north to south. As the latter plate was particularly curious and interesting from its variety, so this, from its simple and almost uniform character, cannot fail of gratifying the architectural antiquary. The left hand side displays the elevation of the west side of the transept; half of the tower, and a section through the first window and arch of Wykeham's work, in the north aile of the nave; also the form of the arch of that aile, with the clustered pier between it and the nave, the wall and clerestory window above, with the slope of the roofs of the nave and the aile. Beneath the arch of the nave is seen part of the screen to the choir, the altar screen beyond, and the eastern window. The right hand half, or section of the south tran- sept, &c. displays the interior of two floors of the tower, the timber work of the roof, and the whole interior elevation of the east side of the said transept: a. elevation of part of the outside of the tower: b. elevation of two floors of ditto: c. section of the south wall and its window, with the arched gallery, or passage: d. timber work of the roof: [since this plate has been engraved, the draftsman informs me, that the rafters here repre- sented, belong to the north transept, and that the timber work of this is a little varied:] e. small bell turret: f section of the gable: g. of one of the windows, with a passage, or gallery beneath: h. triforium, over the aile: [the draftsman has here again made some mistakes; the upper right hand arch represented flat, should be semi-circular; and its impost moulding lowered: the upper string moulding does not continue through the tall attached columns:] i. screen before the venerable chapel: k. ditto to Silk- stede's: l. chapel called by Dr. Milner the *calefactory*, a place " necessary for preserving fire for the thuribles and censers, that were used in the ancient service, as likewise for the monks to warm themselves in cold weather;" over this aile is a vaulted roof, which the same author says communicated between the dormitories and choir, through which the monks were to pass to perform their midnight service: m. section of window over the aile, and n. ditto from the aile, which plainly shows that it was originally intended to cover the slype, or passage, o. with a sloping roof, now raised over p. which is the present library: q. steps from transept to the south aile: r. section of stalls: s. section of arch under the tower: t. screen to the choir: u. altar screen: w. section of a window of the clerestory of the nave: x. steps to the north aile: y. section of window of the aile and profile of the buttress:

z. door-way to the north transept: *figure* 1. Norman window, filled with mullion and tracery, and the sill lowered: 2. an original window: 3. ditto: 4. a series of four windows to the upper story of the transept: these appear to have been inserted by Prior Silkstede, as his initials T. S. appear on one of the bosses to the cornice, 5. under the parapet: 6. flat buttresses at the angle.

PLATE XXV. Front views of the *Monumental Effigies* of *Edington, Wykeham,* and *Waynflete.* That of *Bishop Edington,* A. lays on an altar tomb, within a stone open screen. The statue is fine in proportion, and has been carefully finished. Its mitre, and episcopal costume, are ornamented with much taste and elegance. Its head rests on two pillows, which were supported by two angels, having censers. The figure appears to have been painted. Round the ledge of the tomb is a perfect inscription, with gilt letters on a blue enamelled ground. Here is no appearance of a crosier.—B. effigy of *Bishop Wykeham* on an altar tomb of white marble; at the feet of the statue are three small figures of priests in the attitude of prayer. Dr. Milner states that these are three monks " of the cathedral, who, accordingly as they were appointed to this office every week, were each of them to say mass in this chapel, for the repose of the souls of Wykeham himself, and of his father, mother, and benefactors, particularly of Edward III. the Black Prince, and Richard II. in conformity with the covenant made for that purpose with the prior and community of the cathedral monastery." The effigy is represented in the " mitre, cope, tunic, dalmatic, alb, sandals," &c. and rings on the fingers. All of these are painted and gilt. His head rests on two pillows, which are supported by angels, and beneath his left arm is a representation of his celebrated crosier, which is preserved in the chapel of New College, Oxford, and of which Carter, in his " Ancient Sculpture," has given an etching. Dr. Milner describes the face as placid and intelligent, and the hands as covered with gloves; but I sought in vain for either   Round the ledge of the tomb is a perfect inscription. C. *Effigy of Bishop Waynflete,* resting on an altar tomb, in his " full pontificals of mitre, crosier, casula, stole, maniple, tunicle, rocket, alb, amice, sandals, and gloves :" the latter are adorned with rosets, but have no rings. Between his uplifted hands is the figure of a heart. The mitre is richly ornamented, and rests on two pillows, but here are no supporters, nor is there any inscription, or brass to the tomb. The face of this effigy, as well as that of Wykeham, has been mutilated and repaired: the portrait, very beautifully engraved, for Chandler's Life of Waynflete, and said to be copied from this statue, is very unlike the original.

PLATE XXVI. Part of *a Tomb and fragments of two Effigies.* A. a mutilated effigy of a bishop, commonly attributed, and with much probability, to *Peter de Rupibus,* who, according to Matthew Paris, " sepultus est autem in ecclesia sua Wintoniensi, ubi etiam dum viverit humilem elegit sepulturem." The style of the mitre, drapery, canopy over head, and ornaments down the sides, are all indicative of the age of Rupibus, who died 1238. B. a broken effigy of a knight, in chain-armour, with surcoat, shield with quarterings, on his left arm, and the right arm directed towards his sword. The head rests on two small cushions, on each side of which is a broken figure of a small angel. At the feet is a large figure of a lion. It will be observed, that the space for the lost legs is very short; but it is so in the statue, which has been finely executed, and is said to represent *William de Foix,* of the princely family of that name, who resided on an estate called Vana, or Wineall, near Winchester. The side of the tomb, A. certainly belonged to the statue, as clearly intimated by the first shield and arms, as well as by the style of the arches, and their crockets and finials. The four other shields are charged with the arms of Leon, England, France, and Castile; to all of which royal families he thus appears to have been allied.

PLATE XXVII. *Elevation of one Compartment of the Nave,* internally and externally. These delineations represent the true forms and proportions of the arches, windows, panelling, columns, &c. and the critical antiquary, who wishes to attain accurate information about the styles and dates of our architecture, will find that it can only be accomplished by means of correct geometrical prints: A. elevation, externally: a. clerestory window, with a label, or weather moulding, terminated with corbel heads: b. pinnacle with panelling, an embattled moulding, crockets, and finial: c. string cornice,

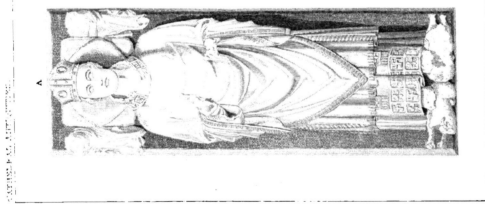

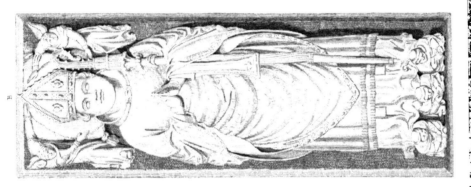

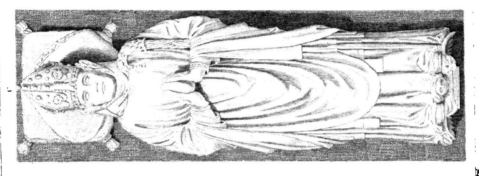

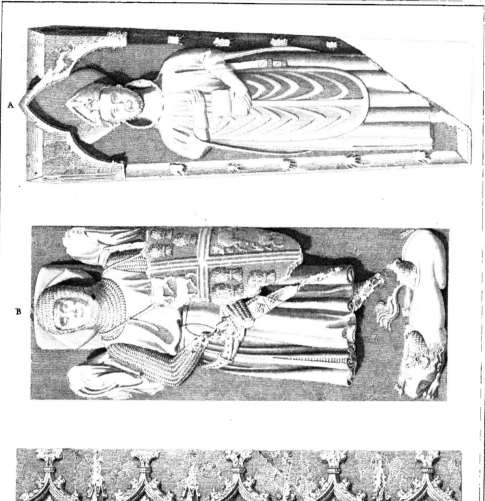

Etched by W. Le Keux from a Drawing by Edw. Blore, for Britton's History &c. of Winchester Cathedral

WINCHESTER CATHEDRAL CHURCH.

Side of an Ancient Tomb & two Effigies.

London Published March 1.1817, by Longman & Co. Paternoster Row.

Printed by Geo. H. Barnett

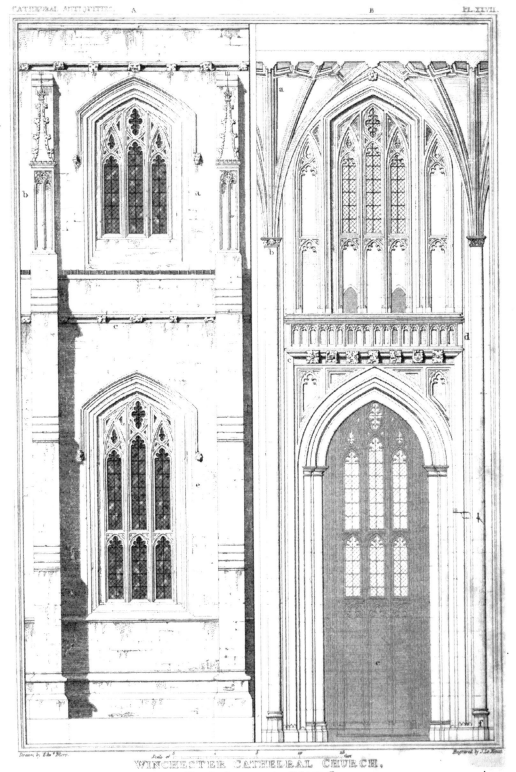

Drawn by Edwd Blore.	Scale of	Engraved by J. Le Keux.

WINCHESTER CATHEDRAL CHURCH,

Nave: *One Compartment, externally & internally.*

London, Published Febʸ 1, 1817 by Longman & Cᵒ Paternoster Row.

Printed by Geo. e Barnett.

London, Published Feb.1.1813. by Longman, & C. Paternoster Row.

Drawn by John Marr.

Etched by R. le Keux

WINCHESTER CATHEDRAL CHURCH.

Elevation, interior & exterior near the Altar

London, Published March 1, 1817, by Longman & C.º Paternoster Row

Printed by Gee & Barnet.

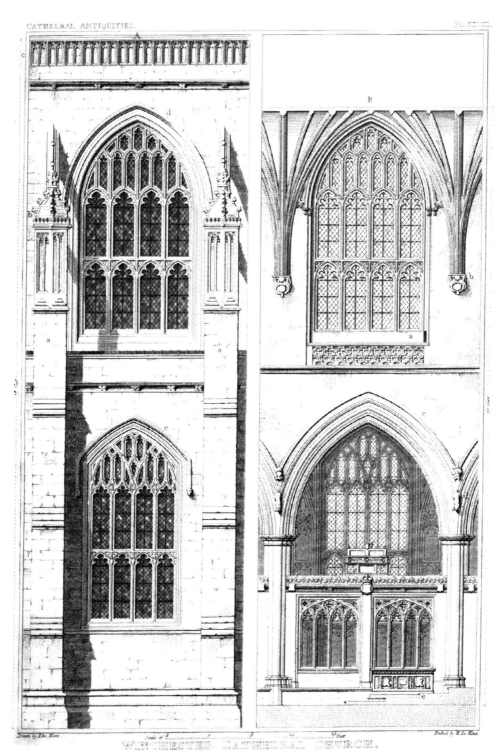

WINCHESTER CATHEDRAL CHURCH.

Elevation interior & exterior near the Altar.

London, Published March 1 1817, by Longman & C.º Paternoster Row.

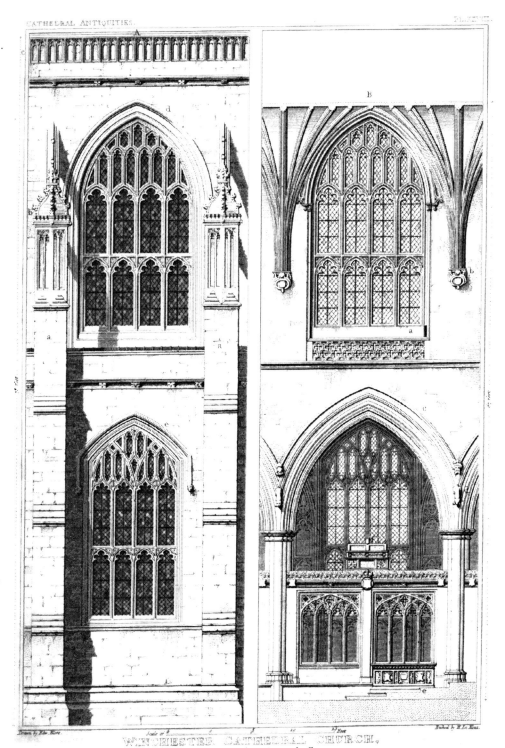

WINCHESTER CATHEDRAL CHURCH,

Elevation interior & exterior near the Altar

London, Published March 1, 1817, by Longman & Co. Paternoster Row.

Printed by Geo. Barnett

WINCHESTER CATHEDRAL CHURCH.
Elevation, interior & exterior near the Altar

London, Published March 1 1817, by Longman & C.º Paternoster Row.

Printed by Cox & Barnett.

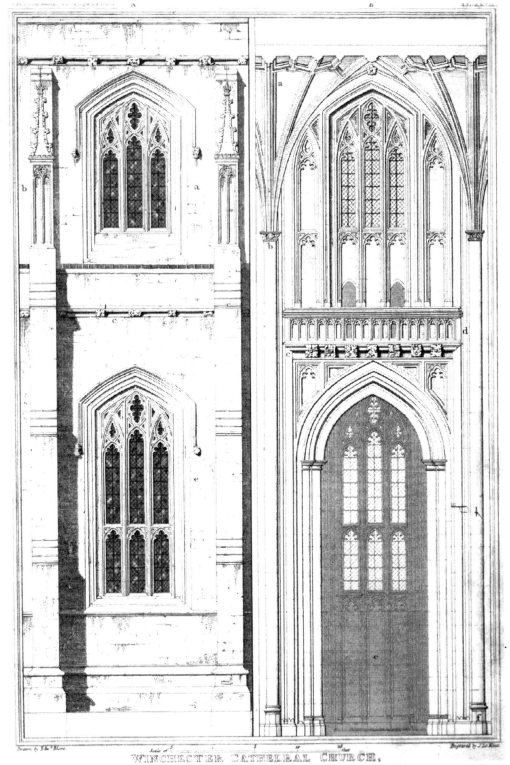

Drawn by Edw.d Blore.

Scale of   5   10   15   Feet

Engraved by J.Le.Keux.

WINCHESTER CATHEDRAL CHURCH.

Nave: One Compartment, externally & internally.

London, Published Feb.y 1.st 1817 by Longman & C.o Paternoster Row.

Printed by Geo. s Barnett

Printed by Cox & Barnett

WINCHESTER CATHEDRAL CHURCH,
Elevation interior & exterior near the Altar.

London, Published March 1 1817, by Longman & Co. Paternoster Row.

with bold roses, and figures. [There should be only three instead of five in this division between the buttresses.] e. window of the aile.—B. elevation, internally: a. groining of the roof, springing from a single shaft, which rises from the floor. Its base is octangular, and the capital is adorned with sculpture of busts, foliage, &c.: c. frieze, charged with large and very finely sculptured bosses of various subjects; among which are the couchant hart, or deer, a man on horseback, the cardinal's hat, busts, the lily, &c. all of which imply that the vaulting and sculpture were raised by different benefactors: d. an open parapet before the old triforium. In the wall beneath the window, is concealed the old Norman semi-circular arch of the triforium, which corresponds in style and height with the same divisions in the transepts: e. panelling under the aile window: f. base of one of the shafts.

PLATE XXVIII. *Elevation of one Compartment of the Presbytery*, externally and internally. A. the exterior, surmounted by an open parapet, c.: a. a. large buttresses, with four breaks, crowned with panelled pinnacles, and ogee, crocketed canopies, or domes, b. The clerestory window, d. as well as that of the aile, e. has three mullions, with a transverse one, and some rich tracery.—B. elevation of one arch, &c. of the interior of the presbytery close to the communion rails: a. upper window, with a gallery, or passage beneath, guarded by a perforated parapet: b. bracket to support the groins of the vaulting, which is of timber: c. arch, with its numerous mouldings, rising on clustered columns of three quarter shafts. From the style of the arch, and its columns, I cannot hesitate in referring the erection of this part of the Church, to the end of Henry the Third's, or beginning of Edward the First's reign: d. grotesque animals at the union of the mouldings: e. steps to the communion table; also the altar tomb, said to belong to Bishop Pontissara, but if so it has been materially altered at the time of putting up the screens. On the top of these screens are six wooden chests, containing some memorials and relics of Saxon monarchs, princes, and other illustrious personages, former patrons of the Cathedral. The names are, *Kynegils, Ethelwulf, Escuin, Kentwin, Elmstan, Kenulf, Egbert, Adulfus, Canute*, and *Emma* his queen, *Alwyn, Wina, Stigand, Rufus, Edmund*, eldest son of Alfred, *Edred*, &c. It may be remarked, that although these names appear on the chests, and we have pretty good authority that the persons they allude to were buried in the Cathedral; yet from the various changes and revolutions that have occurred in this Church, we can scarcely suppose that any remains of them can be identified.

PLATE XXIX. *Arches, and Part of the Tower.* A. elevation of two arches, with the capitals and bases of pilaster columns to the same, placed in a wall under one of the arches of the south transept: B. two other semi-circular arches, ornamented with pilasters and mouldings, like the former, and like those inserted in a wall beneath one of the arches in the west aile of the south transept. Mr. Garbett (*p. 60*) conjectures that the former were erected by Bishop de Blois, to exhibit as specimens of the newly invented pointed arch; but with deference to that intelligent architect, I must contend that the arches, and their members, have been transplanted from some other place, and that in the removal they may have been greatly changed. The pilasters do not appear to belong to the capitals, or to the arches; and certainly the fragment of a pilaster, above the arch-mouldings, B. cannot be regarded as useful, ornamental, or analogous. Besides, if I recollect rightly, there is a finely sculptured bracket of a chained deer, or white hart, the cognizance of John of Gaunt, father of Cardinal Beaufort, inserted in another wall, inclosing the same part of the aile. We may as well attribute this figure to the middle of the twelfth century, as make any inference from the shape of these arches, or their appendages. The arch mouldings are probably of the age of de Blois: but, circumstanced as these fragments are, it would be useless and absurd to deduce from them any criterion as to age and style. Carter, in his " Ancient Architecture," Plate XXXVIII. has given an etching of one of the pointed arches, but so unlike the form, that it appears to be drawn from memory, rather than from the object, or from measurements. He represents each side of the arched line, as a true quarter of a circle, and the arch as forming nearly an equilateral triangle with a line from the capitals. C. elevation of one side of the upper story of the tower, with sections of two of its walls: D. plans of ditto, 1. of the gallery story; and 2. of the story beneath.

PLATE XXX. Two Views of the FONT, which has been called " the *Crux Antiquariorum,* or the puzzle of antiquaries." Its age, and the mean-

WINCHESTER CATHEDRAL CHURCH.

Arches and Parts of the Tower.

London Published March 1 1817 by Longman & C.º Paternoster Row.

Engraved by J Le Keux after a drawing by Edw Blore for Britton's History &c of Winchester Cathedral

WINCHESTER CATHEDRAL CHURCH.

Two Views of the Font.

London, Published Nov. 1 1816 by Longman & Co Paternoster Row.

Printed by Hayward

ing of its rude un-artist-like sculpture, have afforded themes for literary speculation, and will probably long continue enveloped in doubt and obscurity. On such a subject conjecture is likely to play truant: but in the absence of satisfactory history, conjecture must be sometimes allowed, as it leads to investigation, if not immediately to demonstration. The Font is a large square block of black marble, having its four sides charged with sculpture, the angles at the top also ornamented with doves, and cups, and zigzag, and supported by four small columns at the corners, and one larger one in the centre[14]. On two sides are groups of figures, in low, flat relief, with a rude representation in one compartment of a side of a church, and a view of a ship, or boat, in another. Although, as subjects of art, these tablets are beneath criticism, yet as delineations of costume, manners, and implements, they are entitled to special notice and attention. Mr. Gough contends that the sculptures relate to the story of Birinus, and his introduction of Christianity into this province, the death of Kinegils, &c.; but Dr. Milner contends, that they allude to, and are illustrative of, some incidents in the life of " St. Nicholas, Bishop [Archbishop] of Myra, in Lycia, who flourished in the fourth century, and was celebrated as the patron saint of children." As allusive to the figures on one side of the font, it is related that the first act of the saint, who was rich, (a rather un-saintlike circumstance,) was to convey, secretly, sums of gold into the chamber of an impoverished nobleman, who from distress had been tempted to traffic with the chastity of his three daughters, but who, thus enriched, was enabled to apportion each and procure husbands for all. The legend, however, tells us, that " the unostentatious saint" did not perform all his benevolence at once, or in secret, but at three different times, and in the silence of three different nights. On the third occasion, the once poor, but now rich nobleman, watched for and discovered " his unknown benefactor," when falling at his feet—for it seems that he

---

[14] Fonts partly resembling that at Winchester, in size, shape, and material, are still remaining at East-Meon, and at Southampton in Hampshire; and in Lincoln Cathedral. The first is represented and described in the tenth volume of the Archæologia, and the second in Sir Henry Englefield's interesting and erudite little volume, called " a Walk through Southampton."

See also Vetusta Monumenta, *vol.* ii. and Archæologia, *vol.* x. *p.* 184.

O

stole secretly into the chamber—he "called him the saviour of his own and of his daughters souls." This account is not very closely adhered to by the sculptor, for the scene appears to be on the outside of a church, which Dr. Milner identifies as the Cathedral of Myra, and in addition to the saint, the father, and three daughters, here is the figure of a man, with a hawk on his hand.   Let us see if the second side is better elucidated by the legend. It seems to represent three groups of figures and three incidents : 1st. Four standing figures, and the heads of three others prostrate, one of which is dressed as a bishop, whilst another has an uplifted axe, apparently raised to strike at the three heads : 2d, a group, of the said bishop and three other figures, with a fourth laid on his back ; the latter has a cup in his hand, as has also one in the former group: the 3d subject displays a boat, or ship, with a rudder, mast, and three figures in it.   This, Dr. Milner, says represents the saint, on board a vessel bound to Alexandria, and overtaken by a storm, as evinced by the masts being without sails, but which was appeased by the supernatural powers of the saint.   In this voyage one of the mariners fell from the mast and was killed, but was soon restored to life by the miraculous intervention of the Archbishop.   These prodigious works naturally excited much curiosity ; and consequently, on landing, the prelate was visited by great crowds of persons, afflicted with diseases and misery.   The next group therefore shows him in the act of healing the sick ; i. e. of raising two persons, from prostrate attitudes, and astonishing the third person who appears with uplifted hands.   The figure laying on his back, according to Dr. Milner, belongs to a distinct incident and story, but anomalously brought here by the artist.   According to the legendary history of the saint (as written by Jacobus de Voragine,) he appeared, after death, at the bottom of the sea, to a nobleman's son, who was drowned for the sins of his father, and who the Saint conveyed " not only safe to shore, but also to the city of Myra."   In the next compartment the child is led by the Arch-bishop, who is also engaged in the performance of another celebrated act; i. e. rescuing three young men from the impending axe of the public executioner. These three persons had been condemned by the Prefect of the city ; but as St. Nicholas conceived that the sentence was unjust and cruel, be "fled" from Phrygia to Myra, and arrived just at the very critical instant to check the murdering instrument. That such improbable, unnatural, and even impossible stories should have been formerly invented for certain purposes, credited by certain persons, and rendered the themes of literary narrative and disquisition, is most true; that they should be believed by any person who can read and think, in the present age, excites astonishment. For myself, I must candidly acknowledge, that I cannot peruse them without feeling the mingled emotions of pity, regret, and surprise; and cannot write about them without thinking I am trifling with the time and patience of the reader. As forming the subjects of ancient paintings and sculpture, it seems requisite to notice them; and in doing this, I take some pains to be brief. I hope therefore to be pardoned for occupying so much space with the above subject.

Respecting the age of this Font, and its station in a Cathedral Church, I am inclined to think it was the workmanship of Walkelyn's time; when also the font at East-Meon was executed. The style of dress, mitre and crozier, indicates that age. As Cathedrals were not usually furnished with fonts, or their prelates and officers accustomed to perform the sacrament of baptism, Mr. Denne, (in Archæologia, vol. xi.) thinks that as Winchester and Lincoln Cathedrals were provided with fonts they had parochial altars, or chapels.

Some few other objects remain to be noticed. In the south aile of the nave are mural monuments to *Dean Cheney*, and to *Bishop Willis*, the latter of which has a marble effigy of the prelate, reclining on a sarcophagus[15]. In the same aile is a tablet to the memory of Dr. *Thomas Balguy*, formerly an archdeacon of this Cathedral, and distinguished as much for his talents as for his moderation and humility. At one time he was offered the bishopric of Gloucester, but refused the temptation, on account of advanced age and infirmities. His literary works are wholly in the shape of sermons and charges, which were collectively published in 1785. At the advanced age

---

[15] This monument, by R. Cheere, has been praised as a work of art, but the judicious artist and critic will seek in vain for beauty in the execution, or the display of taste in the sculptor. The head is good, but all the rest of the statue is bad. Dr. Milner tells us that the sculptor was silly enough to fret himself to death for having placed the face of the statue towards the west, instead of the east; but this foolish story requires better proof than the gossip of a Cathedral ciceroni.

of 74, this very worthy man died, January 12, 1795. [See Nichols's Literary
Anecdotes, vol. iii. p. 220.] In the nave, near the eighth pillar from the
west end, is a grave stone covering the remains of *Bishop Horne,* who,
according to Dr. Milner, was " the destroyer of the antiquities of his
Cathedral, and the dilapidator of the property of his bishopric[16]." Near
his place of sepulture is that of *William Kingsmill,* the first dean of this
church, who died in 1548. On the north side of the nave reposes *Bishop
Watson,* M. D. who died January 1583-4. Bishops *Walkeyln* and *Giffard*
are said to have been interred in the nave, but there is no memorial to either.
At the west end of the south aile is a small marble slab, to the memory of
James Huntingford, who died September 30, 1772, aged 48. *Bishop
Trimnel,* who died in 1723, is praised in a prolix inscription, as is also his
brother, *Dean Trimnel,* who died in 1729. Attached to the piers near
Wykeham's chantry are marble tablets to commemorate two prebendaries
of this church, and masters of the college, Dr. *William Harris,* who died
in 1700, and *Christopher Eyre,* LL.D. who was interred here in 1743.
Near Bishop Willis's monument is a tablet to record the name and interment of *Dean Naylor,* who died 1739. Another mural monument commemorates Dr. *Edmund Pyle,* prebendary of this Cathedral, who died in
1776. A funeral tablet records some particulars of the family, descent,
public and private virtues of the late *Earl of Banbury,* who died 1793,
and of his Countess, who died 1798. Close to Edington's chantry is a
flat stone, covering the grave of *Bishop Thomas,* with an inscription
detailing his successive preferments; and stating, that he was tutor to the
present afflicted and estimable monarch of these realms.

In the north aile of the nave are interred the mortal remains of a lady,
whose ample benevolence and literary talents must awaken the warmest
emotions of admiration and esteem in the philanthropist and lover of
letters. This was Mrs. *Elizabeth Montagu,* author of an interesting,
eloquent, and discriminating " Essay on the Writings and Genius of
Shakspeare," which attained a sixth edition in 1810; and which displays
the palpable folly and envy of Voltaire's criticisms on our national bard,

---

[16] History, &c. of Winchester, i. 370.

During her life she manifested particular solicitude and generosity towards the poor and unfortunate chimney sweeping boys; and was the founder of a literary society, called " the Blue Stocking Club." Since her decease, which occurred in August 1800, aged 80, four volumes of her letters have been published by her nephew, Matthew Montagu, Esq. which for vivacity, playfulness, ingenious criticism, and versatility of subjects and treatment, are not surpassed by any epistolary writing in the English language. Near Mrs. Montagu repose the relics of Dr. *Joseph Warton,* whose monument, near the entrance to the choir, has been already noticed. This monument was erected by Flaxman, and its expences defrayed by a subscription among the pupils of Winchester College School, to which Dr. Warton had been many years head master. He died Feb. 23, 1800, in the seventy-eighth year of his age. " Biographical Memoirs of Dr. Warton," have been published by the Rev. J. Wooll.

On a flat stone in the north aile is an inscription to Sir *Nathaniel Holland,* Bart. who died, October 15, 1811, aged 76. Among the interments in this pile, is one of a lady whose virtues, talents, and accomplishments entitle her not only to distinguished notice, but to the admiration of every person who has a heart to feel and a mind to appreciate female worth and merit. The lady alluded to, Miss *Jane Austen,* who was buried here, July 1817, was author of four novels of considerable interest and value. In the last, a posthumous publication, entitled " Northanger Abbey," is a sketch of a memoir of the amiable author.

In the south transept are several monuments. One is inscribed with the name of *Colonel Davies,* who met his death at the famous siege of Namur, under King William. Another records the decease of Mr. *Isaac Walton,* the 15th of December, 1683. Few literary works have attracted more publicity than the " Complete Angler," by honest and happy Isaac. His lives of Wotton, Donne, Herbert, &c. are also replete with anecdote and amusement. A full memoir of his life is given in a new edition of " Walton's Lives," by Dr. Zouch, 1807.

At the east end of the south aile is a monument, with a statue, standing, for Sir *John Clobery,* knight, who died in 1687, and who is praised in a long

Latin epitaph, for having been instrumental, with his friend General Monk, in restoring Charles the Second to the throne, and peace to his country[17]. Near this tomb are several flag stones with inscriptions: one records the name of " *the Right Honourable James Touchet, Baron Audley and Earl of Castlehaven,*" who died August 12, 1700; another for the Countess of Exeter, who was interred here in 1663: a third for Lord Henry Paulet, deceased 1672: a fourth to Elizabeth Shirley, daughter of Earl Ferrers, who died in 1740: a fifth commemorates the *Countess of Essex,* who died August 20, 1659, who had married for a second husband Sir *Thomas Higgons,* knight, who pronounced a funeral oration over her grave, in the ancient manner. He died in 1692, and lies near his countess. Another stone covers the grave of *Baptist Levinz,* a prebendary of this church, and Bishop of the Isle of Man, who died in 1692, and is praised in a long Latin epitaph, for abstemiousness, frequent fasting, and " other episcopal virtues." In the north transept are some inscribed slabs; and beneath the organ loft, under the north arch of the tower, is a small inclosed Chapel, or chantry, the walls of which are covered with ancient paintings.

[17] This monument was erected in 1691, and cost £130. It was executed by Sir Wm. Wilson, Knt. the same artist who executed a statue of King Charles II. in the west front of Lichfield Cathedral. The funeral expenses were £125. 5s. 10d.; thus—chanter for office of burial and for the choir, £5. 9s. 4d.; several dues to the church, £8; hanging house and coach with mourning, and the servants to attend, £32. 8s.; torches, bell ringers, &c. £3. 8s.; for rings, £23. 17s. 6d.; for gloves, £16. 15s.; a coffin, £3. 10s.; escutcheons, £12; a gravestone, £20. [Communicated by Wm. Hamper, Esq. of Birmingham, from a paper written by Lady Holte, of Aston-juxta-Birmingham, the daughter of Sir John Clobery.]

Chap. IV.

THE Anglo-Saxon Bishops of Winchester have already been noticed, and some particulars of a few of the earliest of the Norman prelates of that See, have also been mentioned. I now proceed, in conformity with the plan adopted in my History of Norwich Cathedral, to state some anecdotes and characteristic traits of such others of the Bishops of Winchester as have been distinguished by any literary or public works. Of WALKELYN, the first Norman Prelate, some particulars have already been stated. It was the policy, and not without good reason, of the Conqueror to substitute his countrymen and dependents of Normandy, in the room of prelates and other leading churchmen of the old English stock. Walkelyn was his relation and his chaplain; and although inferior in learning to the new archbishop of Canterbury, Lanfranc, (an Italian, but an abbot in Normandy,) he was not without his merits. In 1079, Walkelyn undertook the great work of rebuilding his Cathedral and the adjoining monastery, in a style of architecture till then unparalleled in England; and in 1093, in the reign of William Rufus, the Church was solemnly dedicated. On Walkelyn's death, in 1098, Rufus seized on the bishopric of Winchester, in addition to the other sees he had invaded, and kept possession of it until his untimely end in the New Forest in 1100.

The first act of King Henry the First was to appoint his chancellor, WILLIAM GIFFARD, to the See; but an interval of seven years elapsed before he was consecrated. The cause of this delay was the celebrated controversy which long agitated the church and the state, concerning the conveyance of ecclesiastical investitures from lay persons, by the pastoral staff and the ring; a practice which had been recently condemned by the head of the church. At last, after some years, the contest between the Pope and the King was terminated by a compromise, in which each party

retained possession of his respective rights. Bishop Giffard founded the
Cistercian Convent of Waverley, near Farnham, and erected a palace in
Southwark, afterwards called the Bishop of Winchester's, and also contributed largely to the establishment of the adjoining monastery of regular
canons of St. Mary Overy.

On the death of Bishop Giffard, in 1128-9, the king found means to prefer to the See Henry de Blois, the son of his sister, Adela, by the Earl of
Blois, and who at that time was abbot of Glastonbury. Deeply involved by
family connection, as well as by personal character, in the unhappy contentions for the English crown, which ensued on the death of Henry the
First; the life of Bishop de Blois is much more noticeable in a temporal
and political than in an ecclesiastical point of view. At last his long and
restless occupation of the See of Winchester was terminated by his death
in 1171. The strong fortresses, or castles, erected by him in this city, and at
Farnham, Merden, Waltham, &c. were at once evidences of his wealth and
authority, and of the unhappy spirit and state of the times in which he
lived. Those strong holds have long ceased to be of importance; but one
monument of this prelate's munificence still exists, more congenial with his
spiritual functions, and with the destination of the ample funds entrusted to
his care. To Henry de Blois is this vicinity indebted for one of its principal ornaments, the *Hospital of St. Cross*, founded by him in 1136; an
institution, which, in internal administration, as in structure and appearance, including the additions and improvements introduced by the Cardinal-
bishop Beaufort, has undergone less alteration from its original establishment than any other of a similar nature in the kingdom[1].

According to Rudborne this prelate left certain writings, one concerning
the monument of the renowned British prince, Arthur, discovered at Glastonbury, while Henry was at the head of that abbey: the other related to

[1] The church of St. Cross, has been frequently referred to as containing some curious examples
of ecclesiastical architecture. It is indeed in the whole, and in detail, replete with interest; but
its peculiarities have been either misunderstood or misrepresented. In my *Chronological Illustration* of Ancient Architecture, it is my intention to represent the peculiarities of this building, as
well as those of the Church of Romsey, in this vicinity.

the state of his Cathedral Church, and appears to have been extant in the time of the ecclesiastical historian Harpsfield, towards the close of the sixteenth century.

The vacancy occasioned by the death of Bishop de Blois was not supplied until the end of 1174, by the installation of RICHARD TOCLIVE, alias MORE. In opposition to his repeated engagements, but in conformity with his general practice, the King, Henry the Second, kept the See so long void, in order probably to profit by its revenues; and it was only by the interference of some Cardinals that he granted licence for the election of a bishop to Winchester, and to many other churches which had remained void for some years.

Bishop Toclive was succeeded in 1189 by GODFREY DE LUCY, who not only re-annexed, by purchase from Richard the First, sundry manors formerly belonging to the see, but also restored the navigation of the river Itchen, between Winchester and the Southampton river, and adopted other measures for the general benefit of the city. In the year 1202, this prelate formed a confraternity, or society of masons, and contracted with them for five years, during which time they were to complete certain additions and repairs to the Church. The work then carried on must have been the east end, in which the Bishop was interred in the year 1204, only two years after he had begun his new style of architecture².

During the episcopacy of de Lucy occurred the singular re-instalment of Richard the First, *Cœur-de-lion*, in his regal office. Returning home, less elated with the victories he had achieved in the Holy Land, than depressed by the lawless captivity he had endured under the Duke of Austria, he hardly conceived himself to be a sovereign unless he were again publicly

---

² " Anno 1202. D. Wintoniensis Godfidus de Lucy constituit confratriam pro reparatione ecclesiæ Wintoniensis, duraturam ad quinqua annos completos." Annales Wint. Was not this confraternity a club of *free-masons?*

It must surprise the architectural antiquary to be told, that T. Warton, the historian of English poetry, and the commentator on English Architecture, in his notes to Spenser's " Fairy Queen," refers this very architecture by de Lucy to the time of " the Saxon kings," before the Norman Conquest. See his ".Description, &c. of Winchester," *p. 63.*

crowned and recognised.   The ceremony was performed with great splendour in the Cathedral of Winchester, in the presence of the prelates and
nobles of the kingdom.   But bishop de Lucy was absent ; for Richard had,
on his arrival, resumed the manors he had sold and the castle, on the plea
that the royal demesnes were in-alienable.   We are not, however, informed
that the purchase-money was refunded to the bishop.

Towards the end of 1204, Sir PETER DE RUPIBUS, or DE ROCHYS, was
appointed bishop.   He had been knighted for his military services under
Richard, and hence was generally thought, from his education and habits,
better qualified to command an army than to preside over a diocess.   His
military and political talents were peculiarly serviceable to the Christian
warriors under the Emperor Frederic in the Holy Land, whither our
bishop repaired in 1226.   By him King John was animated to withstand
the Pope's excommunication, and he was afterwards created chief justice
of the kingdom.   On the death of John, from whose vices and mismanage-
ment the nation derived greater and more lasting advantages than from the
virtues and good conduct of many other princes, and on the accession of
his son, Henry the Third, or Henry of Winchester, a child of nine years of
age, the administration of public affairs became almost entirely vested in de
Rupibus.   He succeeded the Earl of Pembroke in the protectorate of the
kingdom ; and even after the young king came of age, his chief reliance for
counsel was on the bishop.   By Matthew of Westminster, however, we
are told that, in 1234, Henry requiring an account of the royal treasures,
the Bishop of Winchester and the treasurer Peter de Rivallis, took refuge
at the altar, and concealed themselves for some time in the Cathedral.
All this notwithstanding, says Matthew of Paris, by his death in 1238,
the whole counsel of England, regal and ecclesiastical, sustained an
irreparable loss.   This bishop's munificence was not confined to the
religious establishments of England: the church of St. Thomas and the
fortifications of Joppa, now Jaffa, in Palestine, were greatly improved at
his expense.

The death of de Rupibus occasioned a violent contest between the king
and the monks of the Cathedral.   Henry was bent on the election of his

queen's uncle, William, chosen bishop of Valence, in France.   The monks, on the other hand, having received an unfavourable report of William, persisted in refusing him, and chose WILLIAM DE RALEY, or RADLEY, then bishop of Norwich.   " When the king heard of their intent," says Godwin, " he was exceeding angry, and made great havock of the bishop's temporalities; swearing he would have his will at last, or they should never have a bishop."   Thinking therefore to satisfy the king, the monks next elected his chancellor, Ralph Nevil, bishop of Chichester: but this election only the more incensed Henry against them.   This indecent contention lasted for five years, although William of Valence, who had occasioned it, had died within a year after it began.   William de Raley withdrew to France, where it became a saying, as Matthew of Westminster reports, that " Henry of England was a coward towards his enemies, and only brave against his bishops."   Being at last reconciled with Henry, the bishop returned to England, and in 1246 performed in his presence the dedication of the royal abbey of Beau-lieu *(de bello loco)* in the neighbouring forest.

The See, vacated by the death of Raley in 1250, was filled by the election of ETHELMAR, or AUDOMAR, the king's half-brother by the marriage of the queen-dowager with Hugh, Earl of March.   Ethelmar had neither morals nor learning, nor the requisite age, nor previous orders in the church, to recommend him for the episcopate; but the monks had suffered too severely in the preceding contest, and were besides convinced that they should not be supported by the Pope against the King; they therefore acquiesced in Henry's proposal.   The presages of Ethelmar's administration were not erroneous, for he conducted himself with so much injustice and tyranny, that he, with his brothers, whose oppressions were felt in other parts of the kingdom, was driven into banishment.   His consecration was deferred for several years; and the monks proceeded, by a new election, to nominate the King's Chancellor, Henry de Wengham, who declined the charge.   At last Ethelmar died at Paris in 1260, on his way to England, having, as some say, succeeded in obtaining consecration at Rome.

The vacant See now became a subject of contention, not between the monks and the King, but among the monks themselves. The Pope, however, set aside the contending candidates, and, by way of *provision*, as it was called, consecrated JOHN OF EXON, or *Oxon*, or *Gernsey*, or *Gerways*, (for so variously is the name written), who had been Chancellor of York. Taking part with the barons against the king, and being suspended by the legate, he repaired to Rome, where he died in 1268; enjoying but a short time the episcopacy, for which he is said to have paid into the court of Rome the vast sum of twelve thousand marks, equal, in effective value, to one hundred thousand pounds of our present money.

John dying *in curia*, or at the court of Rome, the appointment of a successor fell, by the ancient canon law, to the Pope, who translated hither from Worcester NICHOLAS OF ELY, who rebuilt and in 1268, dedicated the church of the original Cistercian abbey of Waverley, near Farnham, previously founded by Bishop Giffard.

" About this time," says Godwin, " the Pope began to take upon him the bestowing of bishoprics for the most part every where. JOHN DE PON-TISSARA, or of Pountoise, in France, was placed by him, upon his absolute authority. He was a great enemy of the monks of his church, whose living he much diminished to increase his own." The most important act of this prelate was the establishment of the college of St. Elizabeth of Hungary, in Winchester, and which was completed in 1301. " The statutes of this college," says Dr. Milner, " prove his zeal for the advancement of piety, morality, learning, and clerical discipline; but they are such as would be thought grievous and impracticable in the present day." [Hist. Win. *vol.* i. 274, from Monast. Aug.]

On the death of John, in 1304, the See was filled by HENRY WOODLOKE, alias DE MEREWELL, in whose time, in 1307, took place the suppression of the celebrated order of the Knights Templars, who had property, and most probably a preceptory, (as their houses were termed,) in Winchester.

The succeeding prelates were JOHN DE SANDALE, REGINALD DE ASSER, JOHN DE STRATFORD, and ADAM DE ORLETON, the latter of whom was translated from Worcester at the end of 1333. He had been one of the most zealous agents of the barons in the first war against Edward the Second. His trial on this account was the first instance in England of a bishop being brought before the ordinary secular tribunal of the country, and this notwithstanding the opposition of the other prelates. The common charge of his being concerned in plotting the death of the unhappy Edward, seems, however, rather doubtful; particularly as Edward the Third, in his complaint to Rome against Orleton, takes no notice of the charge. Whilst he presided at Winchester the monarch removed the woolstaplers from this city to Calais; an event that proved very injurious to our city. Milner calls him " an artful and unprincipled churchman."

WILLIAM OF EDINGTON, appointed to this See in 1345, was the first prelate of the order of the garter, which was instituted five years afterwards. In his capacity of treasurer to the king, he is accused of lowering the intrinsic value of the coin : but the principles on which such an operation of finance must be founded seem to have been very imperfectly understood on both sides of the question. His declining the nomination to the metropolitan throne of Canterbury, is variously explained; although he be reported to have observed, that " Canterbury was the higher rack, but that Winchester was the richer manger." Be this as it may, it appears from Walsingham, copied, though not quoted, by Godwin, that Bishop Edington's executors were sued by his successor, Wykeham, for dilapidations to a great amount. The demands made were for sixteen hundred and sixty-two pounds ten shillings in money, fifteen hundred and fifty head of neat, three thousand eight hundred and seventy-six wethers, four thousand seven hundred and seventy-seven ewes, three thousand five hundred and twenty-one lambs, and one hundred and twenty-seven swine[1]; all which stock, &c. it seems belonged, at that time, to the bishopric of Winchester.

---

[1] Dr. Lowth, who examined the original register, places this number of beasts at the head of the list, and calls them draught-horses instead of swine. The bishop's stock contained doubtless a number of both.

Besides his liberalities to other religious establishments, it appears incontestably from his Will, executed in 1366, the year of his death, that Bishop Edington actually began the great work of rebuilding the nave of his cathedral, and that he allotted a considerable sum of money to carry it on after his death, which happened in October[*].

Of the illustrious successor of Edington, WILLIAM OF WYKEHAM, some notice has already been taken, in reviewing his great works in the Cathedral. It would certainly constitute an interesting theme for biographical disquisition to enter pretty fully into the memoirs of this eminent prelate, architect, and founder: but this pleasure I must deny myself at present, and refer to the ample life of him already written by Dr. Lowth. Intimately connected as he was with this Cathedral and city, endeared as his memory must be to thousands of persons now living, who have profited by his liberal and laudable foundations; he becomes an important and imposing subject. His name is encircled with a halo of merits and virtues; and nothing but praise has been poured forth to embalm his memory. It should, however, be remembered, that panegyric is not history, and that a perfect human being is a *lusus naturæ*. The man who, like Wykeham, amasses an ample fortune, from high political offices, is suspected to want both honesty and integrity: it is generally supposed that he aggrandizes himself at the expense of the country, and that he is influenced more by a lust of power than by the *amor patriæ*. But if, like Wykeham, he bequeaths the whole of his wealth to promote public good and to benefit mankind, he will secure the applause of posterity. Wykeham lived at an important era; was fortunately advanced from poverty to affluence, and from his connection with, and power over the English monarch, was enabled to produce very great effects on the country. His origin was obscure, and his only school education appears to have been derived from the charitable patron-

---

[*] "In this year, 1366, on the 11th day of September, having made his will, Bishop Edingdon directed that out of his estate and goods, money should be expended for completing the nave of the cathedral church of Winchester, which he had begun." *Cont. Hist. Wint. ex registro Langham*, cited by Milner.

age of Uvedale, lord of the manor of Wickham, or Wykeham, a village in Hampshire, the birth-place of our prelate. This gentleman was governor of the castle of Winchester, and placed William at a school in that city; from which he was advanced to be his secretary. At this time Edington was bishop, who introduced Wykeham to Edward III. This splendid monarch soon appreciated and employed the talents of Wykeham. He was first made one of the king's chaplains; and in 1356 was appointed clerk of the king's works in his manors of Hendle and Yestampsted. In the year 1359, he was also nominated surveyor of the works at Windsor, where he appears to have continued engaged till 1373. By his letters patent he was allowed one shilling per day, and two shillings when travelling on business, with an allowance of three shillings a week for a clerk. Soon afterwards he was paid an additional shilling a day. The latter end of the year 1359 the architect's powers were further enlarged, and he was appointed keeper of the manors of Old and New Windsor. " The next year 360 workmen were impressed to be employed on the buildings at the king's wages, some of whom having clandestinely left Windsor, and engaged in other employments for greater wages, writs were issued to prohibit all persons from employing them, on pain of forfeiting all their goods and chattels; and to commit such of the workmen as should be apprehended to Newgate." In 1362, writs were issued to the sheriffs of different counties to impress 302 masons and diggers of stone, for the same works, and in 1363, many glaziers were impressed, and the works at Windsor were carried on till 1373[s]. Wykeham was also engaged in building another royal residence for his monarch and master at Queenborough, in Kent. He was not, however, merely an architect, but was a man of the world and a man of business, and as such was frequently employed by Edward III.

To take holy orders seems always to have been his design; for in all the patents, and even as early as in 1352, he is styled *clericus* (clerk), although he had only received the tonsure, and was not ordained a priest until June

---

[s] Lysons's Berkshire, *p.* 419.

1362, nor even admitted to the low order of alcolythis until the December preceding. His first ecclesiastical preferment was to the rectory of Pulham in Norfolk, to which he received the royal presentation in the end of 1357. Ecclesiastical benefices now flowed in upon him in such profusion, that, as Dr. Milner observes, " we should condemn any other clergyman, except Wykeham, for accepting them ; and we are only induced to excuse him, in consequence of the proofs we have still remaining, that he only received the revenues of the church with one hand to expend them in her service with the other." The yearly value of his benefices amounted to no less a sum than £873. 6s. 8d. money of those days, equal to about £13,100. of present money. So numerous were the offices he held in the church, that it required no small ingenuity to combine them in such a manner that the possession of one should not be incompatible with that of one or all of the others. The advancement of Wykeham in the State kept pace with his preferment in the church. In 1363 he was warden and justiciary of the king's forests south of Trent; in 1364, keeper of the privy seal, and two years afterwards the king's secretary. He is next styled chief of the privy council, and governor of the great council. Froissart, his contemporary, says, " there was at that time a priest in England of the name of William of Wykeham: this William was so high in the king's grace, that nothing was done in any respect whatever without his advice. The king, who loved Wykeham very much, did whatever he desired ; and Sir⁶ William Wykeham was made Bishop of Winchester and Chancellor of England⁷."

While Edward retained the full possession of his faculties, Wykeham continued to enjoy his confidence, but in the close of his reign the jealousy and intrigues of John of Gaunt, Duke of Lancaster, Edward's only surviving son, suspected to entertain some views of ascending the throne in the place of his young nephew, afterwards Richard the Second, succeeded

⁶ The prefix of Sir to the christian name of a clergyman was usual at this time, and implied that he was not graduated in the University; being in orders, but not in degrees ; whilst others, entitled masters, had commenced in the arts.

⁷ Chronicles of England, &c. *vol.* viii. *p.* 385, octavo, 1806.

in undermining the credit of our eminent prelate.   By specious pretences he was removed from his office, his episcopal revenues were sequestrated, and he himself forbidden to approach the court, or the capital.   Previously, however, to the death of Edward, in June 1377, the bishop had in some measure the satisfaction to be restored to the King's wonted favours ; and early after the accession of Richard the Second, all difficulties respecting his affairs were completely removed.   Disengaged, as far as his station would permit from his usual attendance on public business, Wykeham prepared the plans for his two celebrated Colleges, at Winchester and at Oxford.   In 1373 he had opened a school at Winchester ; and the society intended for Oxford was formed several years before the collegiate buildings were commenced.   But these were not the only measures by which his government was distinguished ; for among many others, he sedulously exerted himself to restore the hospital of St. Cross to its original charitable purpose.

To appreciate the character of Wykeham, we must divest ourselves of many notions (prejudices indeed they may justly be termed), resulting from the state of things in our days, compared with that exhibited in England four centuries ago.   Many acts and measures then considered to be beneficial, judicious, and meritorious, may now be regarded in a very different light.   Of the value of the religious, scientific, and eleemosinary institutions of former times, we cannot properly form an adequate estimate : we may, therefore, imagine that much of Wykeham's munificence might perhaps have been better employed.   It must not, however, be forgotten, that monastic institutions, (besides contributing their proportion to the exigencies of the state,) supported the whole body of the poor; exercising hospitality to all, furnishing schools for the gratuitous education of youth, and hospitals for the reception of the sick and infirm.   To the industry of the monks, prior to the discovery of printing, we are indebted for multiplied copies of the scriptures, and of the ancient classic and ecclesiastic writings; and also for the histories and records of past times in general.   It has been unfortunate for Wykeham that he was, more on account of his place and influence than from his personal character, peculiarly obnoxious to a person so powerful as John of Gaunt; but Edward held him in singular favour : for, as Godwin observes, " in the greatness of his authority the king found two notable

Q

commodities, one, that without his care all things were ordered so well as by a wise and trusty servant they might; the other, that if any thing fell out amiss, wheresoever the fault were, he had opportunity to cast all the blame upon the Bishop of Winchester." His Will, made fifteen months before his death, extends to all orders and degrees of men, and answers every demand of piety, gratitude, affection, and charity. Dying in September 1404, he was interred in the chantry he had erected in this Cathedral.

The successor of Wykeham was a prelate of a different description; whose character, through the powerful representations of Shakspeare, seems consigned to perpetual ignominy[s]. This was HENRY BEAUFORT, son of John of Gaunt, Duke of Lancaster, by his third wife, Catharine Swinford. Educated abroad as well as at Oxford, he particularly applied himself to the civil and canon law; studies indispensable for one who, for various reasons, looked forward to a high station in the state as well as in the church. Translated from the See of Lincoln to Winchester, and soon afterwards distinguished by the hat of a cardinal, and involved in the vortex of worldly politics, he at first allowed himself too little time to attend to the spiritual concerns of his diocess. His conduct, however, in his latter days, was very different. He lent to Henry the Fifth, whose treasury was exhausted by his brilliant but destructive successes beyond sea, the prodigious sum of twenty thousand pounds, to ward off a suspected design of appropriating the revenues of the church. Besides the money he expended on his Cathedral, and on various other religious and charitable establishments, he greatly enlarged the usefulness of the hospital of St. Cross, and erected the principal part of the domestic buildings now existing.

Having filled the See of Winchester forty-three years, Beaufort gave place to WILLIAM OF WAYNFLETE, so named from his birth-place in Lincolnshire. To Wykeham's colleges at Winchester and Oxford, he was indebted for his education. Become master of the former, he was engaged by Henry the Sixth to take the same charge of the new institution at Eton. The revenues of Winchester enabling him to carry into effect the project he had for some time contemplated, he commenced his noble institution of

[s] Our bard, appears to be supported by the accounts of Hall, Holinshed, and other old English Chroniclers.

the College of St. Mary Magdalen, in Oxford. Attentive to whatever could promote the views of his new establishment, Waynflete, preparatory to a visit to it in 1481, sent thither a very large number of volumes; eight hundred as some say, which had issued from presses already established in England, as well as on the Continent, or works still in manuscript. Besides the college at Oxford, Waynflete founded a free-school in his native town, and was a benefactor to Eton College, and to his Cathedral of Winchester. Respecting the general character of Waynflete, his biographer, Dr. Chandler, observes, that in the course of his researches, he had met with no accusation of, or reflection on him. Humane and benevolent in an uncommon degree, he appeared to have no enemies but from party, and even those he disarmed of their malice. The prudence, fidelity, and innocence which preserved him in the waves of inconstant fortune are justly the subject of admiration.

Waynflete lived to behold the restoration of the house of Lancaster, in the person of Henry the Seventh; when dying in the year 1486, the king had an opportunity of promoting to Winchester a prelate possessing his high regard. This was PETER COURTENEY, of the family of that name established in Devonshire; a prelate of respectable character, but still more distinguished by his descent from the house of Courteney in France, which sprung from two kings of that country; Robert, who died in 1031, and Lewis Le Gros, or the Sixth, who reigned till 1137. Of this family one branch engaged in the Crusades and became Counts of Edissa, in the east; another, established in France, furnished three Emperors to Constantinople, and continued to be ranked among the Princes of the blood royal, until it was resolved, in late times, to limit that distinction to the descendants of St. Lewis, or the Ninth. The third branch passed into England in the beginning of the reign of Henry the Second, and soon rose to rank and opulence by inter-marrying, at different periods, with the royal family.

The next bishop of Winchester was THOMAS LANGTON, removed hither from Salisbury, a prelate described by Anthony Wood as a second Mecænas, on account of the protection he afforded to literature and learned men. On the death of Morton, Archbishop of Canterbury, he was actually elected to succeed him, but a few days afterwards was carried off by the plague, and was buried in the curious chapel already described.

His successor, RICHARD FOX, had long been the confidential friend and minister of Henry the Seventh, who successfully employed his talents in sundry negotiations with foreign princes. In recompense, he was appointed Bishop of Exeter, retaining still his other offices of privy seal and secretary of state. From Exeter he passed first to Bath and Wells, and thence to Durham, where he displayed his munificence and architectural taste. But in order to have him nearer the court, Henry removed him to Winchester, and even selected him to be sponsor at the baptism of the young Prince, afterwards Henry the Eighth; to whom he subsequently acted as one of the leading counsellors, with equal zeal as when he served his father. Of his retirement from court, in the young king's time, various causes are assigned. It was after this event that he planned the munificent foundation of Corpus Christi College in Oxford. The original purpose of this college was to provide monks for the service of his Cathedral; but, dissuaded from this purpose by a friend, who, notwithstanding the bishop's long and intimate acquaintance with the court, had penetrated deeper than himself into Henry's schemes respecting monastic institutions, he founded the college for the education of secular clergymen. He also provided it with some of the most celebrated scholars of the age, among whom may be named John Lewis Vives, and Reginald Pole, afterwards the celebrated cardinal. Dying in 1528, the bishop was buried in the exquisite chantry he had erected in his Cathedral.

On the death of Bishop Fox, the See of Winchester devolved to the mighty cardinal, THOMAS WOLSEY, who had now engrossed the favour of Henry the Eighth, and obtained some of the richest benefices of the church. At first introduced to the tyrant by Fox, to counterbalance the influence of the Earl of Surrey, afterwards Duke of Norfolk, he soon rose superior to his opponent and to his patron himself. The history of Wolsey, independently of the part he took in public affairs, is little more than a list of promotions, following one another with a rapidity equally alarming to the courtiers, and invidious in the eyes of the people. Of this distinguished prelate and politician, we are furnished with ample memoirs in a large folio volume, by Fiddes; and recently in a new life of him, by Mr. Galt. In my account of York Cathedral, I shall have occasion to make a few remarks on his character.

From the death of Wolsey, Winchester was without a bishop for nearly four years, when the vacancy was filled by STEPHEN GARDINER, who was brought into notice by Wolsey, but who owed his preferment to his readiness to promote and justify every project of the king. Being appointed at the moment when the dispute concerning the ecclesiastical supremacy of the crown was at its utmost height, Gardiner joined the two metropolitans, and some other prelates, in acknowledging Henry to be the supreme head of the church of England. This measure was soon followed by the suppression of the religious houses throughout the kingdom, by which Winchester suffered greatly, both in condition and outward appearance. Notwithstanding his submissive conduct, during the life of Henry, and his taking out a new license to govern his See on the accession of Edward the Sixth, Gardiner resisted all further changes in religion until the young king should be of age, and was therefore by the protector, Seymour, committed to the tower. At last he was declared to be no longer prelate of Winchester, and Dr. JOHN POYNET was appointed in his place; who was the first bishop consecrated according to the new ordinal. On the accession of Mary to the throne, Gardiner was reinstated in his See, and, Archbishop Cranmer being a prisoner on a charge of high treason, he officiated at the Queen's Coronation, and at her subsequent nuptials with Philip of Spain. Of the conduct of Gardiner as a bishop and a statesman, the accounts of writers are contradictory and irreconcileable. Whilst the Catholic justifies and applauds him for courage, consistency, and religious integrity, the Protestant represents and censures him for cruelty and unmerciful tyranny.

Of Bishop POYNET who, on the deprivation of Gardiner in the reign of Edward the Sixth, was translated from Rochester to Winchester, little more is known than that he was an early and a strenuous champion for the reformed doctrines. He was also well skilled in various languages, ancient and modern, well read in the fathers of the church, an able mathematician and a mechanist. On the accession of Mary, he, with many other Protestants, withdrew to the continent, not only on account of religion, but, as it is said, because he was suspected of abetting the insurrectionary movements under Sir Thomas Wyatt. He died at Strasburgh in 1556.

Bishop Gardiner was succeeded by Dr. JOHN WHITE, on the condition that he should pay one thousand pounds annually to Cardinal Pole, who complained that his See of Canterbury had been greatly impoverished in the time of his predecessor, Cranmer. He pronounced the funeral discourse on Queen Mary, whom he extolled with great ardour, while he spoke of her successor, Elizabeth, with extreme coldness. Refusing to take the new oath of supremacy, he was of course, in June 1559, declared to have forfeited his bishopric.

The See of Winchester again remained vacant for some time, until the appointment of Bishop ROBERT HORNE, a Protestant divine of great talents, distinguished by his controversial writings, and by the voluntary exile he underwent in the reign of Mary. While Bishop of Durham, he was noted, according to Anthony Wood, as " a man that could never abide any ancient monument, acts, or deeds that gave any light of or to godly religion." To the injudicious zeal therefore of this prelate may be ascribed the havoc made at that period in the Cathedral and in other edifices of Winchester.

The See was next successively occupied by Drs. JOHN WATSON and THOMAS COOPER, both of whom had studied and taken their degrees in medicine. After the latter, Winchester possessed a second WILLIAM WICKHAM, who died in less than ten weeks after his translation from Lincoln. The next Bishop, WILLIAM DAY, dying in the ninth month of his episcopate, was followed by THOMAS BILSON, a native of Winchester and a Wykehamist, there and at Oxford, of whom Elizabeth had a very high opinion. She appointed him of the privy council; and he employed his pen in justification of her interference in the affairs of Scotland, France, and the Low Countries, yet so as to furnish no pretext for resistance, in any case, on the part of her own subjects against himself. " It was written," says Collier, " to put the best colour on the Dutch revolt." Bishop Bilson continued in Winchester for several years after the accession of James the First; but without supporting the character he attained under Elizabeth. His successor, JAMES MONTAGUE, so much esteemed by James as to be chosen the editor of his writings, sat only about eighteen months, and was buried in the Abbey Church of Bath, which he had repaired at a great expence.

By the death of Montague an opening was made for LANCELOT ANDREWS, who had been in succession, Bishop of Chichester and of Ely. The inscription on his monument in the church of St. Mary Overy, in Southwark, notices with peculiar emphasis the distinctions awaiting him in another world, on account of the *celibacy* he had observed in this.

Dr. RICHARD NEILE succeeded Andrews by his fifth translation, and notwithstanding the course adopted by King James in favour of the rigid Calvinists at the synod of Dort, afterwards united with him in embracing the modified system of Arminius. So far did Neile push his animosity against the Calvinists, whom he had deserted, as absolutely, while Bishop of Lichfield and Coventry, to consign one of them to the stake. He perfectly agreed with Archbishop Laud in forwarding King Charles's views of restoring to divine service, and to the churches themselves, some portion at least of their former splendour and majesty; but being again removed to York, the execution of the scheme was left to his successor in Winchester, WALTER CURLE, who made many alterations in his Cathedral.

On the restoration of Charles the Second, Winchester recovered its bishop, after an interval of ten years from the death of Curle, in the person of BRIAN DUPPA, who had been the king's tutor. It was not, however, until nearly two years afterwards that the church of England and its services were properly re-established; an event which the bishop did not live to witness. By his death the See came to GEORGE MORLEY, Bishop of Worcester, "a man," says Wood, "of tried loyalty, and no temporiser, who had learned to shift his principles to be ready for any turn of affairs that might happen, and always to stand fair for promotion." He built the episcopal palace at Winton, in place of the ruined castle of Wolvesey, also repaired the castle of Farnham, and purchased Chelsea-house as a London residence for the bishops of Winchester.

Dr. PETER MEWS, the successor of Morley, had served in the royal army during the rebellion, and, retiring into Holland on the king's death, returned with Charles the Second, who advanced him to the See of Bath and Wells, and afterwards to Winchester. He signalized himself at the battle of Sedgemoor, where he commanded the artillery: nor was he less valued for his integrity and hospitality than for his loyalty and prowess.

The succeeding prelate, Sir JONATHAN TRELAWNEY, had been raised to the See of Bristol by James the Second ; but in 1688, opposing the king's declaration of liberty of conscience, he was, with his metropolitan and five other prelates[9], committed to the Tower; from which, however, they were, by the sentence of a jury, soon after liberated. Joining heartily in the revolution, he was, by William and Mary, made Bishop of Exeter, and in 1706 was promoted to Winchester.

The successors of Bishop Trelawney were Drs. CHARLES TRIMNELL and RICHARD WILLIS, the former translated from Norwich, the latter from Salisbury. In room of the latter was appointed Dr. BENJAMIN HOADLY, who had previously occupied the Sees of Bangor, Hereford, and Salisbury. This prelate will long be remembered in the church of England from engaging warmly in the celebrated Bangorian controversy. In consequence of the notions maintained by Bishop Hoadly, the government, it is believed, resolved to dissolve the convocation of the clergy ; and since that time, although regularly assembled on the opening of a new parliament, it has never transacted any business.

On the death of Bishop Hoadly, his present Majesty translated from Salisbury to Winchester Dr. JOHN THOMAS, who had been his preceptor, and who, dying in 1781, was succeeded by the present venerable prelate the Hon. BROWNLOW NORTH, then Bishop of Worcester, and brother of the late Lord North, afterwards Earl of Guildford.

---

[9] These were, Sandcroft, Archbishop of Canterbury ; Kenn, Bishop of Bath and Wells; Turner, of Ely; White, of Peterborough; Lloyd, of Norwich; and Frampton, of Gloucester.

END OF ACCOUNT OF BISHOPS.

A Chronological List of the Bishops of Winchester,

WITH

CONTEMPORARY KINGS OF ENGLAND AND POPES.

No.	BISHOPS.	Consecrated or Installed	Died or Translated	Buried at	Kings.	Popes.
	DORCHESTER.	**Anglo-Saxon Dynasty.** From	To		**WEST SAXONS.**	
1	Birinus	 635	 650	Dorchester	{ Kinegils ...... } { Kenewalsh ... }	Honorius I.
2	Agilbert	 650	See divided........ 660	————	Kenewalsh	St. Martin I.
	WINCHESTER.					
1	Wina...	 660	{ Expelled .... 666 } { Died .... 675 }	Winchester	Kenewalsh	Vitalian.
2	Eleutherius	 670	674	Winchester	Kenewalsh	Adeodatus.
3	Hedda	 676	.... July 7, 705	Winchester	Ina	Domnus.
	SEE DIVIDED.					
4	Daniel. See again divided	 706	{ Resigned .... 744 } { Died.............. 745 }	————	Athellard............	John VII.
5	Humfred	 745	754	————	Cuthred	St. Zachary.
6	Kinebard	 755	780	————	Cuthred............	Stephen III.
7	Athelard	 780	Canterbury........ 793	————	Sigebert	Adrian.
8	Egbald	 793	795	Winchester........	Kenewulph	Adrian.
9	Dudda	 795	797	Winchester........	Kenewulph	Leo III.
10	Kinebert........................	 797	————	Winchester........	Kenewulph	Leo III.
11	Almund........................	 808	————	Winchester........	Kenewulph	Leo III.
12	Wighten	 814	————	Winchester........	Egbert	Stephen V.
13	Herefrith	 827	 834	Winchester........	Egbert	Valentine.
14	Edmund	 834	————	Winchester........	Egbert	Gregory IV.
15	Helmstan	 835	 837	Winchester........	Egbert	Gregory IV.
16	St. Swithun	 838	 862	Winchester........	Egbert	Gregory IV.
17	Alfrith, or Adferth	 863	Canterbury........ 871	Canterbury........	Ethelred	Nicholas I.
18	Dunbert....	 871	879	————	Alfred	Adrian II.
19	Denewulf, or Denulf........................	 879	————	————	Alfred	John VIII.
20	Athelm	 887	————	————	Alfred	Stephen VI.
21	Bertulf	 892	 899	————	Alfred	Formosus.
22	Frithstan	 905	{ Resigned........ 931 } { Died .... 932 }	Winchester........	Edward	Sergius III.
23	Brinstan	 931	 934		Athelstan............	John XI.
24	Elphege, the Bald	 934	 951	Winchester............	Edmund	John XI.
25	Alfsin, or Elsin	 951	Canterbury........ 958	Winchester............	Edgar	Agapetus II.

R

No.	BISHOPS.	Consecrated or Installed	Died or Translated	Buried at	Kings.	Popes.
		From	To			
26	Brithelm	 958	 963	————	Edward Mart......	John XII.
27	Ethelwold.....................	 963	...Aug. 1, 984	————	Ethelred II....,......	Benedict V.
28	Elphege II..................... ..	 984	Canterbury........1006		Ethelred II........	John XIV.
29	Kenulph	1006	...—.....1008	Winchester......	Ethelred II........	John XVIII.
30	Brithwold or Ethelwold........	1008	1015			Sergius IV.
31	Elsinus or Eadsinus	1015	Canterbury........1038	Canterbury	Canute..............	Benedict VIII.
32	Alwyn	1038	1047	Winchester......	{ Harold I. } { Hardicanute }	Benedict IX.
33	Stigand	Elmham 1047	{ Canter' cum .....1052 } { Died ....1069 }	Winchester...	{ Edward Conf. } { Harold II. ....}	Damasus II.

Norman Dynasty.

No.	BISHOPS.	Consecrated or Installed	Died or Translated	Buried at	Kings.	Popes.
34	Walkelyn.......	1070	.... Jan. 3, 1097-8	Winchester......	William I. II.......	Alexander II.
35	William Giffard	{ Appointed ....1100 } { Consecrated ....1107 }	.............Jan. 25, 1128-9	Winchester......	Henry I...........	Paschal II.
36	Henry de Blois	...............Nov. 17, 1129	.... Aug. 6, 1171	————	{ Henry I. } { Step. Hen. II. }	Innocent II.

Saxon Line Restored.

No.	BISHOPS.	Consecrated or Installed	Died or Translated	Buried at	Kings.	Popes.
37	Richard Toclive, alias More ...	.... Oct. 6, 1174	1189	Winchester......	Henry II............	Alexander III.
38	Godfrey de Lucy.....................	.... Nov. 1, 1189	{ ..... Sept. 11, } 1204 { ..... Dec. 2, }	Winchester......	Richard I., John...	Clement III.
39	Sir Peter de Rupibus	.... Sept. 25, 1205	............June 9, 1238	Winchester......	John, Henry III...	Innocent III.
40	William de Raleigh	Norwich 1243	.... Sept. 1250	Turon	Henry III.........	Innocent IV.
41	Ethelmar	{ Elected ....1250 } { Never Consecrated }	1261	{ Paris: Heart in } { Winchester.....}	Henry III.	Innocent IV.
42	John of Exon, or Oxon	1261	.............Jan. 20, 1267-8	{ Viterbium, Italy } { Waverley: Heart }	Henry III.	Urban IV. .
43	Nicholas of Ely	.... May 27, 1268	.... Feb. 12, 1279-80	{ in Winchester..}	Henry III. Edw. I.	Gregory X.
44	John de Pontessara	.... June, 1282	............Dec. 4, 1304	Winchester......	Edward I............	Martin IV.
45	Henry Woodelock, or De } Merewell ....}	.... May 30, 1305	.........June, 29, 1316	Winchester	Edward I. II.	Boniface VIII.
46	John De Sandale..................	Elected .... Aug. 5, 1316	.... Nov. 1319	{ St. Saviour's, } { Southwark ..}	Edward II...........	John XXII.
47	Reginald De Asser	...........Nov. 16, 1320	...........Apr. 12, 1323	Avignon..............	Edward II.	John XXII.
48	John De Stratford	...........June 26, 1323	Canterbury, Nov. 3, 1333	————	Edward II. III...	John XXII.
49	Adam De Orleton	Worcester, Dec. 1, 1333	...........July 18, 1345	————	Edward III........	Benedict XII.
50	William Edington	1345	...........Oct. 7, 1366		Edward III...	Clement VI.

Lancastrian Line.

No.	BISHOPS.	Consecrated or Installed	Died or Translated	Buried at	Kings.	Popes.
51	William Wykeham ...... }	1367	.........,.....Sept. 27, 1404	Winchester............	{ Ed. III. Ric. } { II. Hen. IV... }	Urban V.
52	Henry Beaufort, Cardinal......	Lincoln, March 14, 1405-6	...............April 11, 1447	Winchester............	Henry IV. V. VI.	Gregory XII.

York Line.

No.	BISHOPS.	Consecrated or Installed	Died or Translated	Buried at	Kings.	Popes.
53	William Waynflete, alias Patten	.... July 30, 1447	..............Aug. 19/11, 1486	Winchester............	{ Hen. VI. Ed. } { IV. V. Ric. III. }	Nicholas V.

Union of York and Lancastrian Families.

No.	BISHOPS.	Consecrated or Installed	Died or Translated	Buried at	Kings.	Popes.
54	Peter Courteney	Exeter,...Jan. 29, 1486-7	....Sept. 22, 1492	Winchester......	Henry VII.........	Innocent VIII.
55	Thomas Langton	Sarum.....June, 1493	...........Jan. 27, 1500	Winchester......	Henry VII.........	Alexander VI.
56	Richard Fox.....................	Durham.....Oct. 17, 1500	...........Sept. 14, 1528	Winchester......	Henry VII. VIII.	Alexander VI.
57	Thomas Wolsey, Cardinal	With York, Apr. 11, 1529	.... Nov. 29, 1530	Leicester..............	Henry VIII..	Clement VII.

No	BISHOPS.	Consecrated or Installed	Died or Translated	Buried at	Kings.	Popes
		From........................	To			

Reformation.

No	BISHOPS.	Consecrated or Installed	Died or Translated	Buried at	Kings.	Popes
58	Stephen Gardiner............	.... Dec. 5, 1531	{ Deprived..........1550 } { Restored..........1553 } { Died...Nov. 12, 1555 }	Winchester.............	{ Henry VIII. } { Edw. VI........ }	Clement VII.
59	John Poynet	Rochester, Mar.23,1551-2	.... April 11, 1556	Strasbourg	Edward VI. Mary	———
60	John White	Lincoln.....May 31, 1557	Deprived..........1560		Mary	———
61	Robert Horne	.... Feb. 16, 1560-1	............June 1, 1580	Winchester.............	Elizabeth.	———
62	John Watson	..........Sept. 18, 1580	.........Jan. 23, 1583-4	Winchester.............	Elizabeth.............	———
63	Thomas Cowper	Lincoln...Mar. 23, 1583-4	....April, 29, 1594	Winchester.............	Elizabeth.............	———
64	William Wickham	Lincoln...Feb. 22, 1594-5	............June 12, 1595	{ St. Saviour's, Southwark...... }	Elizabeth.............	———
65	William Day	.... Jan. 25, 1595-6	.... Sept. 20, 1596		Elizabeth.............	———
66	Thomas Bilson....................	Worcester, May 13, 1597	............June 18, 1616	Westminster.............	Eliz. James I.......	———

Union of English and Scotch Crowns.

No	BISHOPS.	Consecrated or Installed	Died or Translated	Buried at	Kings.	Popes
67	James Montague	Bath&Wells, Oct. 4, 1616	...... July 20, 1618	Bath	James I.............	———
68	Lancelot Andrews	Ely .... Feb. 25, 1618-9	....Sept. 21, 1626	{ St. Saviour's, Southwark...... }	James I. Charles I.	———
69	Richard Neile	Durham ...Feb. 7, 1627-8	York.............Oct. 1632	York	Charles I...........	———
70	Walter Curle	{ Bath and Wells, Nov. } { 16, 1632 }	1647	Subberton, Hants......	Charles I.	———
71	Brian Duppa	Sarum.........Oct. 4, 1660	.... March 26, 1662	Westminster...........	Charles II..........	———
72	George Morley	Worcester, May 14, 1662	...... Oct. 29, 1684	Winchester...........	Charles II..........	———
73	Peter Mews	{ Bath and Wells, Nov. } { 22, 1684 }	................Nov. 9, 1706	Winchester.............	{ James II. } { Will. Mary } { Anne........... }	———
74	Sir Jonathan Trelawny, Bart. .	Exeter......June 21, 1707	.... July 19, 1721	In Cornwall	Anne, George I....	———
75	Charles Trimnell	Norwich...Aug. 19, 1721	1723	Winchester.............	George I.	———
76	Richard Willis	Sarum ....Sept. 21, 1723	..................Aug. 1734	Winchester.............	George I. II.......	———
77	Benjamin Hoadley	Sarum ....Sept. 26, 1734	1761	Winchester.............	George II.	———
78	John Thomas.	Sarum 1761	 1781	Winchester.............	George III..........	———
79	Brownlow North............ .,...	Worcester 1781	———	———	George III....... ..	———

Chronological List of Priors and Deans of Winchester.

No.	PRIORS.	Appointed.	Died or removed.	No.	PRIORS.	Appointed.	Died or removed.
1	Devotus, or Denotus.	2nd Cent. Abbot or Prior		25	Andrew of London	1256	Deposed 1261 or 2
2	Brithnoth[1]	963	Ely 970	26	Ralph Russel		Died 1265
3	Brithwold, or Ethelwold	970	Bishop 1006	27	Valentin	1265	{ Resigned 1267, Restored 1276
4	Elfric, or Alfric	1006	Archbishop of York 1023	28	John de Dureville	1276	Died Dec. 1278
5	Wulfsig[2]		Died 1065	29	Adam de Farnham	1278 or 9	Died 1284
6	Simon, or Simeon	1065	Ely 1080	30	William II. de Basynge	1284	Resigned 1284
7	Godfrey	1080	Died 1107	31	William III. de Basynge	1284	Died 1295
8	Geffry, or Geoffry I.	1107	Deposed 1111	32	Henry Woodelock, or Merewell	1295	Bishop 1305
9	Geffry II	1111	Abbot of Burton 1114	33	Nicholas de Tarente	1305	Died 1309
10	Eustace, or Eustachius	1114	Died 1120	34	Richard de Enford	1309	
11	Hugh	1120		35	Alexander Heriard		Died 1349
12	Geffry III		1126	36	John III., or de Merlow	1349	1361
13	Ingulphus	1126	Abbot of Abingdon 1130	37	William IV. Thudden	1361	Laid aside
14	Robert I.	1130	{ Bishop of Bath and Wells, 1135 or 6	38	Hugh II., or de Basyng	1361	Died 1384
15	Robert II.[3]		Abbot of Glastonbury 1171	39	Robert IV., or de Rudborne	1384	Died 1394
16	Walter	1171	Do. Westminster 1175 or 6	40	Thomas Nevil, or Nevyle	1394	
17	John		Died 1187	41	Thomas Shyrebourne		
18	Robert III. surnamed Fitzhenry	1187	Abbot of Burton 1214	42	William Aulton		Died 1450
19	Roger	1224		43	Richard Marlburg	1450	Died 1457
20	Walter II.		Died 1239	44	Robert Westgate	1457	1470
21	Andrew	1239		45	Thomas III., or Hunton	1470	1498
22	Walter III.[4]		Resigned 1247	46	Thomas IV., or Silkested	1498	Died 1524
23	John de Canz, or Chance	1247	{ Abbot of Peterborough 1249	47	Henry Brook	1524	
24	William Tanton	1249	{ Abbot of Middleton, Dorset 1256	48	William V. de Basynge, or Kingsmill		{ Gave up his Monastery to K. Hen. VIII 1539

DISSOLUTION OF PRIORY—ESTABLISHMENT OF DEANERY.

No	DEANS.	Installed.	Died or removed.	No.	DEANS.	Appointed.	Died or removed.
1	William Basyng[5]	March 28, 1540	Died 1543	12	Alexander Hyde, LL.D.[11]	Aug. 8, 1660	Bish. of Sal. Dec. 3, 1665
2	Sir John Mason, Kt. M.D Layman[6]	Oct. 9, 1549	Resigned 1553	13	William Clark, D. D.	Feb. 11, 1665	Died 1679
3	Edmund Steward, LL. D.	March 22, 1553	1559	14	Richard Meggot, D. D.	Oct. 9, 1679	Died 1692
4	John Warner, M. D.	Oct. 15, 1559	Died March 21, 1564	15	John Wickart, D. D.	Jan. 14, 1692	Died 1721
5	Francis Newton, D. D.[7]	March 21, 1565	Died 1572	16	William Trimnell, D. D.	Feb. 16, 1721	Died 1729
6	John Watson, M. D.	Feb. 14, 1572	Bishop 1580	17	Charles Naylor, LL. D.	May 7, 1729	Died June 28, 1739
7	Lawrence Humphrey, D.D.	Oct. 24, 1580	Feb. 1, 1589	18	Zachary Pearce, D. D.	Aug. 4, 1739	Bishop of Bangor 1748
8	Martin Heton, D. D.[8]	March 20, 1588	Bishop of Ely, Feb.3, 1599	19	Thomas Cheney, D. D.	March 25, 1748	Died Dec. 27, 1768
9	George Abbot, D. D.[9]	March 6, 1599	{ Bishop of Litch. and Cov. Dec. 5, 1609	20	Jonathan Shipley, D. D.	1760	Bishop of Landaff 1769
10	Thomas Morton, D. D.[10]	Jan. 3, 1609	Bishop of Chester 1616	21	Newton Ogle, D. D.	Oct. 21, 1769	Died 1804
11	John Young, D. D.[10]	July 8, 1616		22	Robert Holmes[12]	Feb. 22, 1804	Died 1805
				23	Thomas Rennel, D. D.[13]	Dec. 9, 1805	

[1] See a particular account of him in Bentham's History, &c. of Ely.
[2] It is supposed there were one or two Priors between him and Elfric, whose names are lost.
[3] Rudborne, Hist. Maj.
[4] Milner says he was deposed by bishop William de Raley. Hist. Winchester, 196.

[5] Surrendered Nov. 15, 1539, was installed, according to charter, May 22, 1544, and henceforth called William Kingsmill, D.D.
[6] He was bred a layman.
[7] Storer's list says 1570.
[8] See Bentham's History of Ely.
[9] Afterwards promoted to London and thence to Canterbury.

[10] Afterwards promoted to Litchfield and Coventry, and thence to Durham.
[11] See History, &c. of Salisbury Cathedral.
[12] Gents. Mag. 1805, Part II p. 1086.
[13] This list furnished by the present learned Dean, who is also Master of the Temple in London.

A

List of Books, Essays, and Prints,

THAT HAVE BEEN PUBLISHED RELATING TO

WINCHESTER CATHEDRAL;

ALSO A LIST OF

ENGRAVED PORTRAITS OF ITS BISHOPS.

THIS LIST IS SUBJOINED TO GRATIFY THE BIBLIOGRAPHER, THE CRITICAL ANTIQUARY, AND THE ILLUSTRATOR; AS WELL AS TO SHOW, AT ONE VIEW, THE SOURCES WHENCE THE CONTENTS OF THE PRECEDING PAGES HAVE BEEN DERIVED, AND THE FULL TITLES OF THE WORKS REFERRED TO IN THE NOTES.

DIOCESS, SEE AND CHURCH, &c.

BEFORE we can write a new book, with any pretensions to novelty, it is necessary to ascertain the contents and character of all preceding publications on the same subject. On many occasions indeed this is not a very easy, or pleasant task : some are rare, some are dogmatical, some are confused and contradictory, some are replete with recondite and abtruse learning, others with fancy, and few or none can be safely relied on for fidelity, and discrimination. Thus the cautious and sceptical writer is compelled to labour through an intricate and thankless labyrinth ; and required to analize, collate, and scrutinise the improbable and contradictory statements that come before him. On no former occasion have I felt this exemplified more forcibly than in respect to the Cathedral now under consideration. The early writers were credulous, and partial, whilst some of those of modern date have come to the task with strong prejudices and predilections ; and from neither of these are we likely to obtain the whole truth. What was formerly written as the history of the church, is only the exaggerated and wondrous account of saints and their miracles, super-natural agency, martyrs, and visions. From such romances it is not easy to extract much authentic history, or probable narration. Most of the oldest chroniclers were bred up and naturalised in monasteries. Hence every thing they relate, as matters of dispute between the clergy and laity, is given with partiality. The first account we find of Winchester Church, is from the pen of *Thomas Rudborne*, a monk of the said church, who is said to have lived in the fifteenth century. He appears to have written a " *History of the Foundation and Succession of the Church of Winchester ;*" also " *Annals*" of the same, from A. D. 633 to 1277. From the latter date, to the Reformation, the succession of Bishops was furnished by another person. These memoirs were given to the public by Mr. Wharton, in " *Anglia Sacra,*" vol. i. in which are the following papers: " *A Letter from the Monks of Winchester, to Pope Alexander II. imploring a restitution of the privileges of which they had been deprived ;* with the Pope's answer, granting their request."—" *Lantfred's Prologue to the History of the Miracles of St. Swithun,*" and " *The Succession of the Priors of the said Church.*" " It is unnecessary to observe," writes Dr. Milner, and very truly, "to persons who are accustomed to the perusal of Monkish Chronicles, that the above-mentioned works can only serve as memoirs for a history, not as histories themselves of the times to which they relate, being upon the whole, vague, jejune, and unconnected, redundant in many particulars, and deficient in others."

The " *Concilia Magnæ Britanniæ*" of Wilkins, folio, 1737, contains the following documents relating to Winchester Cathedral, &c.:—Vol. I. p. 244. Charter of King Edgar to the Monks of the New Monastery, A. 967. Spelman :—p. 240. Laws of the Monastery, given by Edgar, A. 966. ib.—p. 418. Pope Innocent's Letter to Bishop Henry, Legate and Brother to King Stephen, empowering him to hear the complaints of the Monks of Westminster, 1138 :—p. 420, 421. Councils held before the said Bishop. Malmes.—Vol. II. p. 62. Acts against the Confirmation of the Bishop elect. Ex. reg. Peckham: Archbishop's Letter thereon. A. 1281 :—ib. p. 88. Archbishop's proceeding against the Bishop [Pontisara]. A. 1282.—ib. p. 16, 275, 6. Letters from the Archbishop, on his privilege in the election of a Bishop. A. 1303. Ex. reg Winchelsey, fo. 339, 40 :—p. 293. Synodal Constitutions by Bishop Henry Woodloke. A. 1308. Ex. MS. Cotton. Otho. A. 15, fol. 141. a. :—p. 454, Edward

II's Letter to Bishop Henry on Tithes: Answer to the King's Letter. A. 1315. Ex. reg. Woodcock. Winton. Vol. III. p. 26 Archbishop's Mandate to the Bishop to raise a Subsidy. A. 1352. Ex. reg. Islip. 59:—p. 89, Bishop Wykeham's Mandate, ditto. A. 1370. Ex. reg. Winton. Wykeham. 3, 44:—p. 708, Bishop Fox's Letter to Cardinal Wolsey, on the Reformation of the Clergy of England. A. 1527. Ex. Autog. in MS. Cott. Faust. c. vii.—p. 752, Bishop Gardiner's Letter to the King, on his Opinion as to Doctrine. A. 1532. Ex. regis. convoc.—p. 780, The same Bishop's Oath to the King. 1534. Fox's Martyrs, ii. 337.

The new edition of Dugdale's " *Monasticon Anglicanum*," contains notices respecting the See, and Church, from Stevens and Gale;—Short accounts of the Bishops, from Milner, Rudborne, Godwin, &c. up to the time of Bishop Gardiner; also a list of forty-seven Priors; " An Inventory of the Cathedral Church," as furnished to Cromwell. temp. Henry VIII. from Strype's " Memorials of Cranmer;" An Account of the Sale of Church Lands, belonging to this See, during the time of the Civil Wars, Sept. 27, 1646. This work also embraces copies of the following documents: —"No. I. *Ex Annalibus Wintoniensis ecclesie:* MS. in Bibliotheca Cottoniana sub effigie Domitiani, A. 13."—These annals extend only to 1079, when Bishop Walkelyn, re-edified the church from its foundation.—" No. II. *Autographum penes Decanum et capitulum Wintonie*, 1640," being a charter from King Edward, to guarantee the possessions of the church. Dated A. D. 908.—" No. IV. *Ex vetusto exemplari penes Thomam dominum Brudwell.* An. 1652. A similar grant to the former, dated 975.—" No. V. *Sanctus Edelwoldus factus est episcopus ab Edgaro rege.* Ex historia de primis fundatoribus Abandoniensis Cenobii in Bibliotheca Cottoniana, sub effigie Claudii, B. vi. fol. 85. a." An account of the translation of Ethelwold, from the abbacy of Abingdon, to the See of Winton, with the appointment of Osgar, to the former, in 963.—" No. VI. *Fundatores principalis Cathedralis ecclesie sancti Swithuni Winton* Lel. Col. vol. i. p. 613" [428], with lists of Kings, Bishops, and Saints buried in the church.—" No. VII. *Innocentii Charta.* Ex. Chron. S. Swithini Winton, p. 8:" being grants of lands, and churches, to the Prior, and Monks.—" No. VIII. *Alia ejusdem Papæ Innocentii bulla,* ibid." On the same subject.—" No. IX. *Charta Edgari Regis pacifici, pro renovatione terre de Chiltecumbe, et pro introductione Monachorum,* ib. p. 10." —" No. X. *Carta de Hursbourne Edwardi Senioris.*"—" No. XI. *King John's Charter, allowing certain Duties to be collected on the River Itchin, by the Bishop of Winchester.* Appendix to Milner's History of Winchester, from Trussel's MSS."—" No. XII. *Charta Edgari regis, qua nullos unquam fuisse perhibet in Wintoniensi hoc cœnobio Monachos ante hos quos ipse jam introduxit a Monasterio Abingtoniensi.* Wilkinsii Concilia, vol. i. p. 244."—" No. XIII. *Acta contra Confirmationem electi Winton. Episcopi.* [1281.] Ibid. vol. ii. p. 62 Ex. reg. Peckham, fol. 13, b."—" No. XIV. *Archiepiscopi Cantuar. literæ de eodem.* Ibid. ibid."—" No. XV. *Archiepiscopi Cantuar. processus contra episcopum Winton.* Ibid. vol. ii. p. 88. Ex. reg. Peck. fol. 16. a." The three last documents refer to the election of Richard More, Archdeacon of Winton, who was chosen Bishop by the Monks, and approved by the King; but was strongly opposed by Peckham, Archbishop of Canterbury, on account of his having held a plurality of benefices: he was finally rejected by the Pope.—" No. XVI. *Episcopi Winton. mandatum pro subsidio regio colligendo et solvendo.* Ibid. vol. iii. p. 89. Ex. reg. Winton. Wykeham. 3 part, fol. 44."—" No. XVII. *Bulla Urbani Pape Quinti super administratione ecclesie Winton.* E. Registro Wykeham. Part I. fol. 1." This instrument is directed to William of Wykeham, Archdeacon of Lincoln, administrator of the spiritual and temporal concerns of the church of Winton, requiring him to provide pastors for the vacant churches, and to supply all deficiencies in the administration of the See.—" No. XVIII. *Bulla domini Pape directa domino episcopo Wintonien.* E. Registro Wykeham, part tert. a fol. 135." Pope Gregory here announces, that he has received ambassadors from the Kings of England, and France, for concluding a peace between them; and calls upon the clergy of England, for a subsidy to defray the expences which the holy see had sustained in the war.—" No. XIX. *De Cantaria Wilhelmi Wykeham Episcopi Wynton.* Ex Libro evidentiarum ecclesie cathedralis Winton, No. I. fol. 18." Specifying the several masses and services to be performed in St. Mary's College of Winchester.—" No. XX. [Bibl. Cotton. Cleop. E. iv. 8 pag. 258. a.] Com. South. *Valor omnium et singulorum, castrorum, honorum, maneriorum, terrarum et tenementorum ac aliarum possessionum quarumcunque; nec non omnium et singulorum proficuum p. roven. de spiritual. et jurisdictionibus spiritual. pertinen. sive spectan. tam episcopatui Winton. et monaster. sancti Swithini, Winton, predict. quam omnibus et singulis aliis monaster. priorat. archidiaconat. colleg. rector. vicar. cantar. ac liberis capellis, nec non omnibus aliis promotionibus spiritual. in com. prediot. prout valent communibus annis.*"

" *The History and Antiquities of the Cathedral Church of Winchester* : containing all the Inscriptions upon the Tombs, and Monuments : with an Account of the Bishops, Priors, Deans, and Prebendaries; also the History of Hyde Abbey. Begun by the Right Honourable HENRY, late EARL of CLARENDON, and continued to this time, by SAMUEL GALE, Gent. Adorned with Sculptures. London, printed for E. Curll, at the Dial and Bible, against St. Dunstan's Church, in Fleet-street, M.DCC.XV." Octavo. Some on large paper. Some copies have a reprinted title-page, with the following imprint :—" London, printed for W. Mears, at the Lamb, without Temple Bar, and J. Hooke, at the Fleur-de-luce, against St. Dunstan's Church, in Fleet-street, MDCCXXIII."—*Upcott.*

LIST OF PLATES, by V. dr. Gucht, except 13, 15, 16, and 17.—1. View of the Cathedral, folded, 2, 3, 4, 5, 6. Five Plates of the Font.—7. The Entrance to the Choir, the work of Inigo Jones, folded.—8. The Chests of the West Saxon Kings, &c. on the North Wall of the Presbytery, and the Tomb of William Rufus, before the Altar, folded.—9. No title; but showing the south side of Fox's Chantry.—10. " Tomb of Bishop Wainfleet."—11. " Tomb of Richard, son of William the Conqueror."—12. " Monument of Richard, Earl of Portland," folded.—13. " Tomb of William Wyckham, Bishop, Founder of Winchester College," *Hulsbergh,* sc.—14. Slab, with Arms for Baptista Levinz, Bishop of Sodor and Man.—15. " Monument and Statue of Sir John Clobery."—16. " Monument of John Nicholas, S. T. P." Prebendary of Winton.—17. " Monument of William Harris, S. T. P." Prebendary of Winton.—18. Seals of the Cathedral, and of Stephen Gardiner, Bishop. These plates are not only bad specimens of art, but extremely inaccurate and unsatisfactory. The most useful part of this volume, is the list of charters in the tower relating to the churches, &c. of Winchester; and the collection of monumental inscriptions contains some that have been since destroyed.

" *A Description of the City, College, and Cathedral of Winchester.* Exhibiting a complete and comprehensive Detail of their Antiquities and Present State. The whole illustrated with several curious and authentic Particulars, collected from a Manuscript of Anthony Wood, preserved in the Ashmolean Museum at Oxford; the College and Cathedral Registers, and other Original Authorities, never before published." 12mo. pp. 108. London, no date. [" Price one shilling."] 18 pages are appropriated to the city; from 22, to 68, to the College; thence to 108, to the Cathedral. There is no name or date to this vade mecum, but the Rev. R. Mant, in his Memoirs of T. Warton, ascribes it to that learned historian of English poetry, and supposes it was published in two small tracts, about 1754. " A surreptitious and imperfect edition of it," says Mr. Mant, " was soon afterwards printed by W. Greenville, Winchester[1]."

" *The History and Antiquities of Winchester,* setting forth its Original Constitution, Government, Manufactories, Trade, Commerce, and Navigation; its several Wards, Parishes, Precincts, Districts, Churches, Religious and Charitable Foundations, and other Public Edifices : together with the Charters, Laws, Customs, Rights, Liberties, and Privileges of that ancient City. Illustrated with a variety of Plates." In two volumes 12mo.—vol. i. pp. 237; exclusive of preface, title, and dedication, vol. ii. pp. 299. Winton, 1773. These volumes contain twelve " cuts," and, besides accounts of the city, cathedral, &c. comprehend histories of the College, and of St. Cross. They are evidently compiled by a person, or by persons, who were little versed in topographical and antiquarian literature. Formerly they were said to have been written, or arranged, by the Rev. Wm. Wavel, but some descendants of that gentleman, have disavowed his connection with the work. Dr. Milner, in his preface, shows that the work is replete with " flagrant errors," enough " to require a whole volume to detect them all."

" *The History, Civil and Ecclesiastical, and Survey of the Antiquities of Winchester.* By the Rev. John Milner, M. A. F. S. A." In two volumes, 4to. Winchester, 1798. " Vol. I. being the Historical Part, Vol. II. the Survey of the Antiquities." With plates, and a plan of the city.

A second edition was published in 1809, with considerable additions, and a copious postscript, in which the several strictures contained in the reviews, &c that had been published on the work, are detailed and discussed. 12 copies printed on large paper of the first edition, and some large paper of the second. The following extract from the advertisement will explain the difference between the two editions :—" A copious postscript is annexed to the present edition, in which the several strictures contained in the reviews and other works that have been published on the subject of the history, are detailed and discussed. Several considerable additions are interspersed throughout the work, and

---

[1] This work, says Dr. Milner, " is exceedingly defective and erroneous:" some instances of which the Doctor points out in the tenth page of his preface.

particularly amongst the notes ; one of these contains observations upon a work lately published, in two octavo volumes, called *British Monachism*. Another addition consists of a whole new chapter, being a survey of the most remarkable modern monuments in Winchester Cathedral.

" Certain notes, which seemed to be of little importance, are abridged or omitted in this edition, and the whole preface to the second volume is left out, as the substance of it is contained in the postscript.

" The style of the whole work has been carefully revised, and (it is hoped) considerably improved.

" Lastly, the plates have not only been re-touched, but also corrected and improved. Three new plates are also given in this edition."

This work, from the principles and opinions of the author, occasioned a warmly contested controversy, between himself, Dr. Sturges, Dr. Hoadley Ashe, and several anonymous writers in the Antijacobin Review, British Critic, Hampshire Repository, and other critical journals. These disputes were chiefly on matters of opinion,—on subjects that always have been, and ever will be unsettled and uncertain; and therefore liable to sectarian interpretation. " Zealous bigots" have always injured the cause of truth and history, by partial and intemperate representations. On Dr. Milner's work, the following comments have been recently published :—

" T. Warton, in his Description of Winchester, had said of the college library, that it was made by Warden Pinke, which Milner, vol. ii. p. 144, calls an unpardonable error, in a Wykehamist. Dr. Milner's is a good and useful history in many particulars; but he should have been aware of charging any other writer with errors. In this very sentence he has made an error of the same sort, and as great as that which he censures. T. Warton was not a Wykehamist, as any member of the college could have told him; and with as little trouble he might have learned what ground there was for saying that Warden Pinke made the library ; for, though T. Warton's expression was careless, yet in the main it was true. In the same part of the volume, besides this mistake concerning T. Warton, there are left, between Dr. M. and his printer, more errors than pages for a dozen together. Again, p. 141, Dr. M. says of Warton's book, that the errors of the press are exceedingly numerous and gross, particularly in the epitaphs. Now he himself has given eight of those epitaphs, in each of which, taking one with another, he has made two errors ; and in vol. ii. p. 27, he has printed William of Wykeham's epitaph, in which he has made as many faults as lines." History of Winchester College, with plates, 4to. 1806, p. 40, published by Mr. Ackermann, London.

" *Reflections on the Principles and Institutions of Popery*, with reference to Civil Society and Government, especially that of this kingdom ; occasioned by the Rev. John Milner's History of Winchester. In Letters to the Rev. John Monk Newbolt, Rector of St. Maurice, Winchester. By John Sturges, LL.D. Prebendary of Winchester, Chancellor of the Diocese, and one of his Majesty's Chaplain's in ordinary." 8vo. Winchester, pp. 298.

" *Letters to a Prebendary :* being an Answer to Reflections on Popery, by the Rev. J. Sturges, LL.D. Prebendary and Chancellor of Winchester, and Chaplain to his Majesty ; with Remarks on the Opposition of Hoadlyism to the Doctrines of the Church of England, and on various publications occasioned by the late Civil and Ecclesiastical History of Winchester. By the Rev. John Milner, M. A. F. S. A." 4to. Winchester, 1800, pp. 300. Six editions of this have been since printed in octavo.

In the " *Hampshire Repository*," vol. i. and ii. is a Review of Milner's " History and Antiquities of Winchester." Its beauties and defects are pointed out, and its errors refuted. The conductor of the Repository defends himself from the censures and reflections cast upon him by Mr. Milner. Dr. Sturges's " Reflections on Popery," and Mr. Milner's Answer thereto, are also briefly noticed.

" *An Historical and Critical Account of Winchester Cathedral* ; with an engraved View and Ichnographical Plan of that Fabric, extracted from the Rev. Mr. Milner's History and Antiquities of Winchester. To which is added, a Review of its modern Monuments." 1801, 8vo. pp. 148.

" *The History and Antiquities of the Cathedral Church of Winchester*," in sixteen pages, with eight prints, and a plan, constitute the fourth number of " A Graphic and Historical Description of the Cathedrals of Great Britain," 1813, demy 8vo. 7s. 6d., super-royal 8vo. 12s., and quarto 1l. 1s. The plates are, a ground plan :—Pl. 1, " great west door-way," or porch :—Pl. 2, west front, from north west angle :—Pl. 3, view of the north side of nave, west side of north transept :—Pl. 4, distant view from the ruins of Wolvesey :—Pl. 5, N. E. with houses in the foreground :—Pl. 6, S. transept, upper part of the choir, &c.—Pl. 7, part of S. side of nave, and W. side of transept :—Pl. 8, interior view of N. transept.

In the second volume of "*Vetusta Monumenta*" are long accounts, by R. Gough, of the Chantries of *Cardinal Beaufort, Bishop Waynflete*, and *Bishop Fox*; with anecdotes of each prelate, and six engravings by Basire, from drawings by Schnebbelie, representing the said chantries, and some of their ornaments. Had these plates been accurately drawn and engraved, they would have proved highly interesting and valuable; but the slovenly style in which they are executed, seems rather to tantalize than gratify our curiosity. In Gough's Sepulchral Monuments, are similar accounts.

ACCOUNTS OF BISHOPS.

"The Life of William of Wykeham, Bishop of Winchester; collected from Records, Registers, Manuscripts, and other authentic Evidences. By·Robert Lowth, D. D. Prebendary of Durham, and Chaplain in ordinary to his Majesty." 8vo. pp. 404, 1758. This is the title to the first edition: a second was printed in the following year, "with additions," and a third in 1777. Dr. Milner says, that this volume "contains much useful information, and also many mistakes."

"Historica Descriptio complectens Vitam ac Res Gestas Beatissimi viri Gulielmi Wicami quondam Vintoniensis Episcopi, et Angliæ Cancellarii, et Fundatoris duorum Collegiorum Oxoniæ et Vintoniæ. Oxoniæ, e Theatro Sheldoniano, An. Dom. 1690. 4to. 137 pages." With the arms of William of Wykeham to front the title-page.

N. B. The author of this Memoir, was Dr. Thomas Martin, Chancellor of this Diocese, under Bishop Gardiner, and it was first printed in 4to. in 1597.—Gough.

"The Life of William Waynflete, Bishop of Winchester, Lord High Chancellor of England, in the Reign of Henry VI. and Founder of Magdalen College, Oxford: collected from Records, Registers, Manuscripts, and other authentic Evidences. By Richard Chandler, D. D. formerly Fellow of that College." 8vo. pp. 428, London, 1811, with Plates.

ENGRAVED PORTRAITS OF THE BISHOPS OF WINCHESTER.

1. WILLIAM OF WICKHAM: *Houbraken*, sc. l. h. sh. from a picture in Winchester College. Illust. Head.—Whole length, from the picture in Winchester College, *Grignion*, sc.—tomb of. sh. by J. K. Sherwin.—Large 4to. New College, Winton, *J. Faber*, f.—From effigy on his tomb. *Grignion*.—One by Parker. *Granger and Bromley*.

2. HENRY BEAUFORT, at Mr. Walpole's, done for Harding's Shakspeare, by *J. Parker*. *Granger*.

3. WILLIAM WAYNFLETE: *Houbraken*, sc. 1742, from a print at Magdalen College, Oxford, large h. sh. Illust. Head.—Gulielmus Patten, alias Waynflete, Mariæ Magdalen College, Oxon, 1459, *J. Faber*, f. large 4to. mez.—One by Parker. *Granger and Bromley*.

4. RICHARD FOX: Johannus Corvus Flandrus faciebut, *Vertue*, sc. 1723. In Fiddes' "Life of Cardinal Wolsey," from the original picture at C. C. C. Oxon.—*G. Glover*, sc.—*Sturt*, sc.—A small oval, for Dr. Knight's "Life of Erasmus."—One of the founders, *J. Faber*, fc. large 4to. mez. 1516.—One by Parker. *Granger and Bromley*.

5. THOMAS WOLSEY: Holstein, p. Faber, sc. One of the founders, 4to. mez —A label from his mouth, inscribed "Ego meus et rex," 4to.—Two, with and without arms, prefixed to his "Life" by Cavendish. *Elstrake*, sc. 4to.—Head by *Loggan*, in Burnet's "History of the Reformation."——in Holland's "Heroologia," 8vo.—*W. M. (Marshall)* sc. small in Fuller's "Holy-state."—P. Fourdriner, sc. h. len. h. sh. in his "Life," by Fiddes, fol. 1724.——*Houbraken*, sc. Illust. Head. in the possession of Mr. Kingsley.——*Desrochers*, sc. 4to.—inscribed *C. W. Vertue*, sc. a small oval.——One by Parker[2]. *Granger and Bromley*.

6. STEPHEN GARDINER: in Harding's Shakspeare, 1790, *W. N. Gardiner*, by Gunst. *Bromley*.

7. ROBERT HORNE: inscribed "Stephen Gardiner," fol. *Holbein. R. White. Granger and Bromley*[3].

---

[2] "There is no head of Wolsey which is not in profile." Bromley.

[3] "It seems now pretty clear, that this print is really the portrait of Bishop Horne, as appears from the figure of the person, and the arms, "three bugle horns." Edmund Turnor, Esq. of Sackville-street, who did me the honour of communicating this article, purchased at a sale, a portrait of a bishop, with the arms of the See of Winchester impaled with *B. a cross, or; between four birds heads, erased of the second, in the centre of the cross a cinque-foil, gules*: which were the arms granted to Bishop Gardiner. Mr. T. afterwards compared it with an undoubted portrait of that bishop in the lodge of Trinity-Hall, in Cambridge, (whereof Gardiner was some time master,) and found it to be the same countenance exactly, but in better preservation. *Bromley*.

8. JAMES MONTAGUE : 4to. S. Pass.——one 12mo.——one by Elstrake——one 24mo. by S. Pass, 1617——one in the " Heroologia," copied. *Bromley.*

9. LANCELOT ANDREWS : *J. Payne,* f. 1632, Frontispiece to his " Exposition of the Ten Commandments," fol. This is copied by *R. White,* in 12mo.—— *R. Vaughan,* sc. 4to.——*Hollar,* f 1643, 12mo. In Bishop Sparrow's " Rationale of the Common Prayer," in which are several other heads by *Hollar.*—Prefixed to his " Preces Privatæ," *D. Loggan,* sc. 1675, 12mo.—Frontispiece to his " Devotions," 18mo.—By *Simon Pass,* without his name, 1618, 4to.——By *Simon Pass,* looking to the left, 1616, 4to. *(rare),* inscribed " Episcopis Winton."——From his Monument at St. Mary Overies, two different aspects. *Granger and Bromley.*

10. WALTER CURLE : fol. *T. Cecil,* sc ——Another by *Droeshout.* *Bromley.*

11. BRIAN DUPPA : *R. W. (White),* sc. before his " Holy Rules and Helps of Devotion," &c. small 12mo. 1674 ——A Portrait of him at Christ Church, Oxford. *Bromley.*

12. GEORGE MORLEY : *P. Lely,* p. *R. Tompson,* exc. large h. sh. mez.—*Lely,* p. *Vertue,* sc. 1740. In the collection of Gen. Dormer, at Rowsham. Illust. Head.—Sitting in a chair, h. sh. mez.——A portrait of him at C. Ch. Oxford.—*Bromley and Granger.*

13. PETER MEWS : *D. Loggan,* ad vivium del. et sc. h. sh.——Two oval prints, *no name.*—A portrait at St. John's College, Oxford. *Bromley.*

14. JONATHAN TRELAWNEY : portrait at C. Ch. Oxford. *Bromley.*

15. CHARLES TRIMNELL : mez. *J. Faber. Noble, Bromley.*

16. BENJAMIN HOADLEY : æt. 67, 1743, sitting in robes, sh. *W. Hogarth,* p. *B. Baron,* sc.—æt. 80, Profile prefixed to his " Works," fol. 1773, *N. Hone,* p. *J. Basire,* sc. 1772.——Oval, in a canonical habit, *J. Faber,* mez.——Altered to a bishop's, with Simon's name.—— Canonical habit altered to a bishop's, la. fol. *G. Vertue,* sc.—Oval, in a canonical habit, 4to. mez.—One by *M. V. Gucht,* 8vo. oval in wood before his " Life." *Bromley.*

17. JOHN THOMAS : standing in the robes of the garter, mez. *B. Wilson,* p. *R. Houlston,* sc. 1771.

PORTRAITS OF DEANS OF WINTON.

1. LAWRENCE HUMPHREY : in the " Heroologia," by *Pass.*——Another in " Boissard." *Bromley'*

2. RICHARD MEGGOT : la. fol. *G. Kneller,* p. *D. Loggan,* sc.——Another la. fol. *G. Kneller, R. White.*——One prefixed to his " Sermons, 1685, 8vo. *R. White. Bromley.*

3. ZACHARY PEARCE : prefixed to his " Works," 1777, 4to. *Penny,* 1768, *T. Chambars.*—— Three quarters length, sitting, mez. *T. Hudson,* 1754, *J. Faber,* sc. *Bromley.*

4. JONATHAN SHIPLEY : oval frame, mez. *J. Reynolds,* p. *J. R. Smith,* sc. 1777.——Prefixed to his " Works," 1792, 8vo. *J. Reynolds,* p. *T. Trotter,* sc. *Bromley.*

VIEWS AND PRINTS OF THE CHURCH, AND OF ITS MONUMENTS.

In addition to the prints already specified as belonging to different books, the following have been published :—*South prospect of the Cathedral,* by Dr. King, in Dugdale's Monasticon, vol. i. In Gough's " Sepulchral Monuments," are the following : *Wil. de Basyng's* coffin lid, vol. i. pl. ii. p. 63:—*Inscriptions* from the Church, ib. vol. ii. pt. i. pl. xxxii:—in Carter's " Ancient Architecture of England," the following subjects are represented. viz. *Tomb of William Rufus :—An Arch* in the wall of the west aile of the south transept :—one compartment of the *North Transept,* with details at large :—*Door-way,* formerly in the wall of the south transept :—view of one side of the *Font :*—also elevations of the two sides charged with sculpture, and of the upper surface.—Other prints of this font are given in the " Archæologia," vol. x. also in " Vetusta Monumenta," vol. ii.—A *South-east* view of the *Cathedral,* drawn and etched by J. Buckler, and aquatinted by R. Reeve, was published in 1808 :—a *North-west* view of the *Cathedral,* drawn and etched by J. C. Buckler; and a *South-east* view, by the same artist, are published in No. IV. of " Etchings of the Cathedral, Collegiate, and Abbey Churches."—In Carter's " Specimens of Ancient Sculpture, and Painting," are four etchings of the *Paintings on the Walls of St. Mary's Chapel,* with a long dissertation on the subjects by the Rev. J. Milner.—A view of the *Nave* of the Cathedral, engraved by D. Havell, from a very beautiful drawing by F. Mackenzie, is published in Ackermann's " History, &c. of Winchester College," 4to. 1816.

A CHRONOLOGICAL TABLE

OF THE

AGES AND STYLES OF DIFFERENT PARTS OF THE CHURCH, &c.

Bishops.	Kings.	Temp.	Parts of the Edifice.	Described.	Plates.
Walkelyn......	William I......	1079 to 1093	Crypts under the Presbytery and Ailes, also under de Lucy's work. Part of the Chapter-house, Transepts and Tower, Internal Parts of the Piers, and Walls of the Nave, afterwards cased by Wykeham. Font	57, 8, 9... 70, 77 .... 91, 99, 87 105	II. III. VI. IX. XII. XIII. XXIII. XXIV. XXIX. XXX.
Hen. de Blois	Henry I........	1129	Arches in S. Transept	60, 104...	XXIX.
De Lucy......	Rich. I. John......	1189 to 1205	Chantry Ailes, east of the Altar Screen, with Part of the Lady Chapel, the Two Side Chapels, and Staircase Turrets	60, 97.....	III. VII. VIII. XVII. XVIII. XX. XXIII.
N. Eliensis....,	Hen. III. Ed. I. II.	1280 to 1310	Presbytery from the Tower, to the Altar Screen .... Old Screen, with Niches, &c.........	103	XIII. XXVIII. XXII. XXIII. XXVI.
Edington......	Edward III...	1330	Stalls of the Choir .... West Front, Two Windows on the North, and One on the South ... Edington's Chantry......................	63, 92. ... 64, 88, 89 101	XIII. XIV. IV. V. XI. XXV.
Wykeham.....	Edw. III. Rich. II..	1370 to 1400	Nave and Ailes .... Wykeham's Chantry and Tomb...	65, 75... 102, 91... 101, 93...	III. IX. X. XI. XIII. XXVII. XVI. XVII. XVIII. XIX.
Beaufort.......	Henry IV.	1410	Beaufort's ditto...........................	94.........	XVII. XVIII. XXV.
Waynflete.....	Henry IV.		Waynflete's ditto, and Altar Screen	101, 98... 96, 92...	XV. XVII. XXII. XXIII. XXV.
Courteney	Edward IV...	1480	St. Mary's Chapel, Pulpit...........	67, 76.... 97, 90....	VIII. XX. XXI.
Langton	Henry VII....	1493	Langton's Chapel............	67, 77, 83	XVII. XXI.
Fox	Ditto...........	1500	Fox's Chantry Chapel, Windows of Presbytery and its Ailes, and the Screens....................	67, 94....	VII. IX. XV. XVI. XXII.
Gardiner......	Henry VIII...	1540	Gardiner's Chantry	96.........	XVIII. XXIII. XXVIII.
Rich. Neile...	Charles I.......	1627	Fitting up Altar Screen, Screen to Choir, &c.	80..........	X. XXIV.

List of Prints.

ILLUSTRATIVE OF WINCHESTER CATHEDRAL.

Plates.	Subjects.	Drawn by	Engraved by	Inscribed to	Described.
I	Ground Plan of the Cathedral......	E. W. Garbett	G. Gladwin ...	——	81, 2, 3.
II	Plan and Section of the Crypts, &c.	E. W. Garbett	J. Roffe	——	87.
III	Views of Capitals and Bases of the Nave and Choir	C. F. Porden.	T. Ranson.....		88.
IV	View of the West Front	E. Blore......	J. Le Keux...	Hon. and Rev. Archdeacon Legge...	88.
V	Section and Plan of ditto............	E. Blore......	E. Turrell.....	——	88.
VI	View of the North Transept, &c...	E. Blore......	J. Le Keux...	Sir Thomas Baring, Bart....	89.
VII	View of North Side of Choir, from N. E.	E. Blore......	J. Le Keux...	Rev. Dr. Nott	90.
VIII	View of the East End................	E. Blore......	R. Sands.....	Rev. H. Lee	90.
IX	South Transept, with Ruins........	E. Blore......	R. Sands.....	Rev. Dr. Rennell, Dean of Winchester	90.
X	View of the Nave, looking East....	E. Blore......	—— Edwards	B. Winter, Esq...............	90.
XI	View across the Nave, from N. to S.	E. Blore......	W. Radclyffe	Rev. Archdeacon Hook......	91.
XII	View of the North Transept, looking N. E.	E. Blore......	R. Sands.....	Dr. Powell......................	91.
XIII	View of the Choir, looking West..	E. Blore......	W. Radclyffe	——	91.
XIV	Part of the Stalls of the Choir. For the Title Page	E. Blore.	H. Le Keux...	——	92.
XV	View of the Altar Screen	E. Blore......	H. Le Keux...	Rev. E. Poulter...............	92.
XVI	View of Wykeham's Chantry, &c...	E. Blore......	W. Radclyffe	Warden and Fellows of New College Oxford, and of Winchester College.................	93.
XVII	View of Beaufort's Chantry, with Part of Fox's and Waynflete's...............	E. Blore......	E. Turrell	——	94.
XVIII	Waynflete's Chantry, with those for Chandler and Beaufort...	E. Blore......	J. Le Keux..	President and Fellows of Magdalen College Oxford............	96.
XIX	Groined Roof of Waynflete's Chantry, and Plans of Clustered Columns	E. Blore......	R. Roffe	——	97.
XX	Elevation of Three Compartments on the North Side	E. Blore......	J. Roffe........	——	82, 6, 97
XXI	Carved Wood Work	E. Blore...... ...	E. Turrell	——	98.
XXII	Parts of Altar Screen ; Old Screen ; and Fox's Chantry	E. Blore......	G. Hollis	——	98.
XXIII	Section and Elevation East of the Altar Screen	E. Blore...... .	J. Le Keux...	Rev. F. Iremonger	98.
XXIV	Elevation and Section of the Church and Tower from N. to S.	C. F. Porden.	H. Le Keux...	W. Garbett, Esq.......... ..	99.
XXV	Monumental Effigies of Bishops Edington, Wykeham, and Waynflete	E. Blore......	—— Edwards	——	101.
XXVI	Side of an ancient Tomb, and Two Effigies	E. Blore......	H. Le Keux...	——	83, 102.
XXVII	Nave, One Compartment, externally and internally	E. Blore......	J. Le Keux...	——	102.
XXVIII	Elevation, interior and exterior, near the Altar..........	E. Blore......	H. Le Keux ..	——	103.
XXIX	Arches and Parts of the Tower.....	E. Blore......	G. Hollis	——	104.
XXX	Two Views of the Font	E. Blore......	J. Le Keux...	——	104.

INDEX.

A.

Agilbert, bp. account of, 26.
Alfred, King, crowned in Winchester Cath. 33.
Alfrith, or Adferth, bp. 32.
Altar Screen, Pl. XV.; described, 92; of St. Alban's, 93, n.; Pl. XXII.; described, 98.
Alwyn, bp. account of, 42.
Andrews, bp. 127.
Arches, early pointed with ornaments, Pl. XXIX.; described, 104; semicircular ditto, pointed ditto, 60.
Architecture, Ancient, only to be understood by Plans, Sections, &c. 88.
Asser, Reginald de, bp. 116.
Athelm, bp. 34.
Austen, Jane, 109.

B.

Balguy, Dr. Thomas, 107.
Banbury, Earl of, 108.
Beaufort, Henry, bp. 122.
Beaufort's Chantry, Pl. XVII.; described, 96.
Bertulf, bp. 34.
Bilson, Thomas, bp. 127.
Birinus, extraordinary Miracle of, 23.
———, death of, 26.
Bishops, Seven consecrated in one day, 35.
Bishop's Throne, 76.
Blois, bp. de, 54; Account of, 112.
Brinstan, or Birnstan, bp. 36.
Buttress, Profile and Plan of, Pl. V.; Views of, Pl. VI.; various, Pl. VII.

C.

Calefactory, 100.
Canute, King, 42.
Capitular Chapel, 82.
Cathedral Church begun, 48; converted into a Heathen Temple, 22; fortified, 31; Chapter-house, 83; Choir, 76, 80; described, 91; Crypt, 58, 77; described, 86; Nave, 75; described, 102; Tower, 56, 78; Norman Roof, 57; Exterior described, 73; Interior, 74.
Cathedrals considered as national property, 78, n.;
——— disgraced by trifling tombs, 79, n.
Cerdic, obtained possession of Venta, 22.
Chapter-house, 83; Plan of, Pl. I.; Ruins of, Pl. IX.
Cheney, Dean, 107.
Chests, with remains of Saxon Kings, &c. 103; one of them shown, Pl. XV.
Christianity, conversion of the Britons to, 10.
Choir, 76, 80; View of, Pl. XIII.; described, 91.
Civil Wars between Stephen and Matilda, 54.
Clobery, Sir John, 109.
Cloister Wall, extent of, Plan I.
Columns, Plan of, Pl. I. VI.; one of the Crypts, Pl. II. 3, 6; Clustered, Caps, Bases, and Plan of, Pl. III.; Plans, Pl. XIX.
Cooper, bp. account of, 127.
Cœur-de-Lion, Rich. the First, 54; account of, 113.
Courteney, Sepulture of, 84; bp. account of, 123.

Cross, St., Hospital and Church, 112.
Crypts, 77; Plan and Section of, Pl. II.; described 86.
Curfew Bell first established at Winton, 47.
Curle, bp. 128.

D.

Daniel, bp. 28.
Davies, Colonel, 109.
Day, Wm. bp. 127.
Defects of Exterior, 78.
——— of Interior, 79.
Denewulf, or Denulf, bp. 33.
Dorchester Church, Account of, 24.
Dunbert, bp. 33.
Duppa, bp. 128.

E.

Eadmund, or Edmund, bp. 30.
East End, View of, Pl. VIII.; described, 90.
Edington, bp. account of, 117; Chantry, Pl. XI.
Edington's Effigy, Pl. XXV.; described, 100.
Edward the Confessor, 43.
Edwy, Coronation of at Winchester, 37.
Effigies of a Knight, Pl. XXVI.; described, 102; of a bishop, ditto.
Effigies of Beaufort, &c. 81; Edington, Wykeham, and Waynflete, Pl. XXV.
Egbert, King, crowned King of all Britain at Winchester, 29.
Eleutherius, bp. 27.
Ely, Nicholas of, bp. 116.
Elphege, St. the second, bp. 41.
Elsin, or Alfin, bp. 36.
Emma, Queen, Fiery Ordeal of, 43.
Ethelwold, St. bp. 38.
Ethelmar, bp. Sepulture of, 91; account of, 115.
Exon, or Oxon, bp. 116.
Eyre, Dr. 108.

F.

Foix, Wm. de, Effigy of, described, 102.
Font, two Views of, Pl. XXX.; described, 104.
Fox, bp. his Architecture, 86; Chantry, Pl. XVII.; described, 94; Part of, Pl. XX.; described, 98; Pl. XXII.; described, 98, 99; Account of, 124.
Free-masons, 113.
Frithstan, bp. 36.

G.

Garbett, Mr. his Architectural Account of Winton Cathedral, 55.
Gardiner's Chantry, Pl. XVIII.; described, 96, 99; bp. account of, 125.
Giffard, Wm. bp. 50; account of, 111.
Ground Plan, 81.
Groining of Roofs of Nave and Ailes, Pl. I. and Pl. V.; of Waynflete's Chantry, Pl. XIX.
Guardian Angels, or Portland Chapel, 83.

H.

Harris, Dr. Wm. 108.
Hedda, bp. 28.
Herefrith, bp. slain at Charmouth, 30.

Helmstan, or Helinstan, bp. 30
Hoadly, Ben. bp. 128.
Holland, Sir Nath. 109.
Horne, Robt. bp. 108, 126.
Huntingford, Jas. 108.

I.

Improvements made by Dean and Chapter, 78.

K.

Kenelwalsh, King, founded the See of Winton, 25.
Kenulph, or Elsius, bp. 41.
Kinegils, death of, 25.
Kingsmill, Dean, 108.

L.

Lady or Virgin Chapel, 82; Windows, Plan, &c.
86; Elevation of Pl. XX.; described, 97; Pl.
XXI. p. 98.
Langton Chapel, 77, 83, 96; Wood-work of Pl.
XXI.; described, 98.
————, bp. account of, 124.
Lucius, a British King, enquiry concerning his
history, 12; death of, 14.
Lucy's, bp. de, Architecture, 86; Columns of, 88;
Elevation of, Pl. XX. 97; Section of Three Ailes,
Pl. XXIII.; described, 98; account of, 113.

M.

Mayor appointed, 53.
Mews, bp. 128; Vault of, 83, 87.
Minstrels Gallery, 88; View of. Pl. V.
Misereres, or Seats, 92.
Montague, bp. 127.
Montagu, Eliz. 108.
Monuments and Slabs generally injurious, 79. n.
Morley, bp. account of, 128.
Mullions of Windows, Pl. I.

N.

Nave, 75; Plan of Pier, Pl. III.; described, 88;
View of, Pl. X. XI.; described, 91; Elevation of
one compartment, Pl. XXVII.; described, 102.
Naylor, Dean, 108.
Neile, bp. account of, 127.

O

Orleton, bp. 116; death of, 83.

P.

Panelling over West Front, Pl. IV.
Pinnacles of West Front, Pl. IV.
Pontissara, bp. de, 116.
Portland, Earl of, and Chapel, 83, 87.
Poynet, bp. account of, 126.
Presbytery, 76; Column of, 88; Elevation of one
Compartment, Pl. XXVIII.; described, 103.
Pulpit, 76; Pl. XXI.; described, 98.
Pyle, Edm. 108.

Q.

Quilchelm baptized at Dorchester, 24.

R.

Richard (Cœur-de-Lion) crowned a second time,
54; account of, 113.
Raley, bp. de, account of, 115.
Rufus, Wm. death of, 49; Tomb, 91.

Rupibus, bp. Effigy of, Pl. XXVI.; described, 102;
account of, 114.

S.

Screen to Choir, 80; to Altar, 81; behind Altar,
Pl. XXII.; described, 98.
Silkstede's Chapel, 83; Sepulture of, 85.
Stalls of Choir, Pl. XIV.; described, 92.
St. Paul, doubts of his residence in Britain, 12.
Stigand, bp. 44; death of in Winchester Castle, 45.
Stratford, John de, bp. 116.
Swithun, St. bp. 30; died, 32; tomb of, 85.

T.

Thomas, bp. 108.
Toclive, bp. account of, 113.
Tower, 78; Section of, Pl. XXIV.; described, 100;
Part of, Pl. XXIX.; described, 104.
Transepts, South and North, 76, 80; exterior View
of the latter, Pl. VI.; described, 90; S.Transept,
View of Pl. IX.; described, 90; interior of N.
Pl. XII.; described, 91; West exterior of N.;
described, 99; interior of S. Pl. XXIV.; des-
cribed, 100.
Trelawney, bp. 128.
Tribune, or Minstrels Gallery, 88.
Trimnell, bp. 108; account of, 128.

V.

Venta, Church of, rebuilt, 21; obtained the rank of
a Metropolis, 22.

W.

Walkelyn, bp. 46; account of, 111; curious grant
of Wm. the Conqueror to, 48.
Walton, Isaac, 109.
Warton, Dr. Jos. 109.
Watson, bp. 108, 127.
Waynflete, bp. account of, 122; Chantry, Pl.
XVIII.; described, 96; Roof of, Pl. XIX.; de-
scribed, 97; Effigy of, Pl. XXV.; described, 101.
West Front, View of, Pl. IV.; Section of, V.; de-
scribed, 88, 89.
White, John, bp. account of, 126.
Wickham, Wm. bp. account of, 127.
Wighten, bp. 30.
Willis, bp. 107, 128.
Wina, bp. 27.
Winchester partly destroyed, 52; partly restored,
53; Castle begun, 47; conquered and occupied
by French troops, 54; place of importance at an
early period, 10.
Windows, Plans of five, Pl. I.; Great Western, Pl.
IV.; square-headed ditto; Elevation and Sec-
tion of, Pl. V.; Circular, Pl. VI.; of Nave, Pl.
XXVII.; of Presbytery, Pl. XXVII.; of East
End.
Woodloke, or Merewell, bp. 116.
Wolsey, bp. account of, 125.
Wykeham's Chantry, ill placed and bad in design,
79; Pl. XVI.; described, 93; Architecture of,
Pl. XXIV.; described, 100; Effigy, Pl. XXV.;
described, 101; account of, 118.

ERRATA.

Page 48, line 15, for "*three days*," read *four days and four nights*, as stated by Rudborne, Annales, p. 295.
Page 62, lines 17, 18, &c. omit, and substitute, "the face of the work, as well as the mouldings, are wrought with care and accuracy."

END.

CPSIA information can be obtained at www.ICGtesting.com
Printed in the USA
LVOW111950050412

276370LV00012B/93/P